BUNTIE WILLS: THERAPIST
A MOSAIC

BUNTIE WILLS
THERAPIST

a mosaic

First Published in Great Britain in 1990
by The Buntie Wills Foundation

This edition published in Great Britain in 2016
by Archive Publishing, Dorset, England

© 2016 Archive Publishing

A CIP Record for this book is available from
the British Cataloguing in Publication data office

ISBN 978-1-906289-33-1 (paperback)

www.archivepublishing.co.uk

www.transpersonalbooks.com

Now that my house is burned down
I have a much better view of the moon.

Zen Poem

CONTENTS

INTRODUCTION

Buntie Wills was a psychotherapist and, for some, a spiritual teacher who practised from Landseer Studios at 10a Cunningham Place in St. Johns Wood, London, from the 1950s until her death at the end of 1985.

This is not a definitive book about her therapeutic method. It is a mosaic of personal memories and tributes through which we have tried to capture something of the richness experienced by those who knew her.

The group which has produced this book came together in response to a request in the first newsletter of the new Buntie Wills Foundation. We were self-selected individuals who began meeting in November 1986 for a variety of reasons and with a shared motive – to say thank you.

We faced the seemingly impossible task of creating a book 'by committee' from the many contributions we received. Then the idea of a mosaic was taken up, giving us a way of putting together these pieces to make what we trust has become a whole picture.

We are deeply grateful to have been part of that process. We hope that the book will touch the reader as much as we find its creation has enriched us.

The Books Group of the Buntie Wills Foundation

Peggie Brown	*Charles Chadwyck-Healey*
Annie Elkins	*Lois Graessle*
Vicki Mackenzie	*Mildred Masheder*
Dee Purrett-Smith	*Jean Simpson*
Robert Smith	*Carol Spero*

CONTRIBUTORS

This book has been made possible by contributions from some of the people who knew and worked with Buntie Wills. Several times over the past four years the Books Group sent out requests for remembrances. Some of the pieces we received have been edited to fit the format of the book. It was not intended to alter the meaning and should you feel this has happened in your case, we offer our apologies.

Frankie Armstrong
Di Booth-Jones
Peggie Brown
Melinda Caink
Charles Chadwyck-Healey
Barbara Davis
Mary Edkins
Catherine Ensor
Jane Evans
Ros Finlay
Joan Garrett-Goodyear
Lois Graessle

Gabrielle Boole
Diana Bracebridge
Bridget Browne
Lorraine Craig
Hazel Davies
Eva Davis
Annie Elkins
Mary Ann Ephgrave
Mary Evans
Sanchia Gainsborough
Penny Gill
Tai Chigetsu Hazard

Lindie Jones
Kathleen Browne Kratochwil
Vicki Mackenzie
Jon Maddison
Mildred Masheder
Shauna Mahlo Craxton
Dee Purrett-Smith
Jackie Robarts
Molly Robins
Martin Robinson
M.E.H.S.
Jean Simpson
Carol Spero
Gillian Thoday
Philippa Vick
Patrick Worth
Catherine Yarrow

Hetty Kothari
Meg Leng
Catherine Mackwood
'Maggie'
Noreen Matthews
Eleanor Murray
Jeremy Quin
Alexandra Roberts
Christina Robinson
Gerhard Rosenberg
Philip Seddon
Robert Smith
John Strachan
Susanna Vermaase
Joy Winterbottom
Piers Worth

ACKNOWLEDGEMENTS

We would like to thank those who have helped us to prepare the book for publication: Lorraine Craig, Mary Ann Ephgrave, Joan Garrett-Goodyear, Martin Robinson and Piers Worth for their comments; Claire Massy for administrative help; Geoff Green for design; Alison Moss for supervising the printing; and Tracey Ayre, Lisa Jaglo and Peter Miles for computer support.

We have also appreciated the practical support and encouragement of the Trustees of the Foundation.

The photograph of 10a Cunningham Place is reproduced by the kind permission of the Greater London Photograph Library.

Most of the quotations at the ends of chapters were used by Buntie Wills. We have attributed these wherever that has been possible.

1912 – 1985

I ABOUT BUNTIE

When the Buntie book was first thought of I wrote, as others did, a few paragraphs about what she had meant to me as a life-long friend, which at the time seemed to be all I needed to share. Then, gradually, it dawned on me that as I was the only person who had known about most aspects of her life since she was fifteen I would have to write more, for no-one else was in the position of being able to draw the many threads of her life together. So, I had to start at the beginning.

Buntie – Phyllis as she was then – and I met on our first day at the Willesden School of Art, then in Priory Road, Kilburn in London. This encounter sticks in my memory. I can still visualize her, a sturdy figure with a thickly-freckled face and short dark hair, fully equipped to embark instantly on her life's work: ranged in the pocket of her school blazer were a row of perfectly sharpened pencils, a notebook, a pen, a ruler, in one hand a T-square and in the other set-squares. Nadia, another girl who also became a great friend, and I played the unwise virgins who had come totally unprepared and Buntie, quickly summing up the situation, graciously supplied each of us with a pencil and offered the loan of other equipment if needed. Ungratefully I put her down as smug and awful, but as time passed and first impressions were modified, we all settled down into our particular roles. Buntie's was to become the jester, the one who made us laugh most with her

1

sophisticated jokes – and the one who worked the hardest. She was popular with everyone, students and staff alike, but in general she contrived to evade close contact with individuals.

Almost from the start my friendship with Buntie was threaded with laughter. Humour was part of her nature and something we shared, for we both had mothers who were able to laugh at vicissitudes, in spite of the many tribulations they, and we too, had to face, and our upbringing had a similar light touch. Later, I came to understand that, for Buntie, apparent gaiety was her way of concealing the deep seriousness and vulnerability which she allowed to emerge only in close personal relationship.

In and out of college, work for her was paramount, and she prevailed on me to go in our free time on sketching expeditions into the countryside. I particularly recall a snow-covered sojourn at Kenwood House, trying to draw with frozen fingers details of the facade with its Doric columns while the sky darkened and snowflakes soaked the pages of our sketch books. I was infuriated to have been dragged out there on such a day, the more so because I knew she was right to struggle against inertia and the elements. Later I discovered it was part of her nature to face up to every challenge and one of the reasons why she was so successful in everything she attempted. Such excursions were also the opportunity for her to talk on very serious subjects such as philosophy and ethics: I would have preferred to discuss rather more frivolous topics and could not have been a very responsive companion.

Probably it was during one of these outings that Buntie told me how it came about that she had chosen art as her career. Partly it was due to the influence of her idolised older brother, himself an artist. But also at the age of the thirteen she wrote to Frank Brangwyn, then regarded as the greatest mural artist and etcher of his day and later knighted, saying how much she admired his work and asking for a photograph of himself. He sent her a very handsome one with a letter

2

saying that, 'If you are going to be an artist, you must work very hard from nature and not look too much on the works of man,' with, in his turn, a somewhat peremptory request for a photograph of her. It is unlikely that she would have complied for she was always very shy about her appearance. But he was a romantic-looking man and his name was often woven into the conversation; there is little doubt that his advice influenced her decision.

Later on it emerged that, had Buntie not decided to make art her career, she would have gone on to university to read science. Her annual reports from Hendon County School show that there was no subject at which she did not excel, and they always included impressive comments on her progress and conduct. But once she had decided at the age of fifteen to be an artist, she had taken the money her parents had given her to pay her school fees for the following year and booked herself in at the Willesden School of Art. They did not discover this until some time later, no doubt when enquiries were made about her non-appearance at school. It was quite typical of her to assert her independence in such an unequivocal way.

Once at art school, because she was still under sixteen she was obliged to incorporate an English class into her curriculum, which was how it came about that she was chosen to play the lead in the end-of-term play, as Mrs. Disraeli. Partly perhaps because of the theatrical influence in her family background but also because she did well anything she attempted, she gave a memorable performance, coping coolly with such emergencies as finding her bustle attached to the trellis at the back of the stage from which she had to play a passionate love scene; and then, flinging herself in despair on to a sofa, only to find herself gliding across the stage and into the wings. The audience was entranced, and she received the ensuing laughter and applause with admirable aplomb.

Then there was the annual Fancy Dress Ball. One of my friends and I dressed up as Oxford and Cambridge dolls, the usual Boat Race favours before the war. Wearing huge dark blue and light blue wigs and stiff tulle skirts, we were drawn round the hall in a small rocking boat, an early toy of my brother's. We were a sensation. But we did not win the prize, for behind us walked a small rotund figure in sombre black, the lace-veiled head bearing a jewelled coronet: Buntie – as the widowed Queen Victoria. Needless to say, she stole the scene and won the prize.

After Buntie died a mutual friend at art school wrote to me, reminding me of a project she and 'Phyllis' had undertaken. Maggie wrote, 'About the end of our art school days, my brother took me to his rugger club at Osterley and showed me the dark old wooden pavilion and asked me if I could brighten it up. I was rather appalled, but thought that if only Phyllis would help it could be done. She agreed, and we planned a frieze all round the room and started to work. It took a long time, and she had to come some distance from Golders Green to Osterley – by train and bus and then a long walk – in all weathers. Typically Phyllis did almost all the design work; I merely filled in acres of flat colour. It certainly brightened up the old place. Phyllis was the most obliging person and would do anything she could to help us.

Buntie's firm intention was to earn her own living as soon as possible so that she could be of help to her parents and no longer dependent on them. She worked very hard and within two years had passed the Advanced Drawing Group Examination with distinction, and had assembled a portfolio full of diverse examples of the kind of work she had discovered would be in demand in commercial art studios. Unknown to anyone, she set off to look for an acceptable job, and almost immediately was snapped up at a display studio run by a despotic but discerning woman – known as Mrs. P. – who thereafter shamelessly exploited her ingenuity and capacity for hard work. Buntie, however, would not allow herself to be exploited for long and bided her time, becoming indispensable and accumulating experience in dealing with a variety of clients, at the same time assembling a more professional portfolio. She was so competent and reliable that when Mrs. P. had to spend a period in hospital she left Buntie in sole charge of the studio and workshop, as several scribbled notes from the sickbed make clear. Then, when the time was ripe, Buntie and three friends who were also desperate to get away from the tyranny of Mrs. P. all resigned at the same time and set up a workshop off the Euston Road under the name of 'Creative Arts.' They had also appropriated some of the most valuable of Mrs. P.'s clients and these provided the basis of the enterprise, which immediately proceeded to flourish.

Her staunchest ally was Phyllis Sale, a delightful character whose generosity together with Buntie's small capital made the move possible, and it was their amicable relationship and the congenial atmosphere they created that impressed me when eventually I joined them there. Later on, before Creative Arts moved to Cunningham Place, she left to settle in the country where Buntie often visited her – I too sometimes – and they remained life-long friends.

During her time at Mrs. P's Buntie had met a brilliant Scandinavian artist who was working in London for a brief period. They had a lot in common, fell in love and talked seriously about marriage. For some time Buntie hovered between acceptance and doubt, but in the end admitted to herself, and to him, how out of place she would feel in a cold and alien climate, away from home and the independence that was so vital to her. At that time we were pursuing our own lives and met only occasionally but when we did meet I was amazed at her transformation from a plump adolescent into a slim and glamorous young woman, wearing make-up and a picture hat. Later she told me she had been living on a diet of dried prunes and had fainted on a bus; she never did things by halves. The glamour burgeoned, but her much-loved man went back to his own country. They wrote to each other for many years and more than once he returned – still full of hope – but in the end gave up and married another.

At this time I was working in a display studio with limited prospects and was looking out for other opportunities, when out of the blue I was offered a job at Creative Arts. It took me some time to make up my mind, knowing it would mean working irregular hours and probably seeing less of friends with other interests. Eventually I decided to go along and see how it would turn out, and moved into an atmosphere of concentrated but fascinating work, lightened by the gaiety and laughter which Buntie always created around her.

Time went by and changes were thrust upon Creative Arts. The workshop was destined for redevelopment, Phyllis Sale moved away to the country, and we three artists who were left had to look for other premises. For some time nothing suitable materialized until an advertisement appeared in a daily paper offering a studio to let in St. John's Wood for a very reasonable rent. Wasting no time we obtained an order to view, and taking in the space, the domed roof and the graceful columns, we all knew instantly that here at Studio E Creative Arts had found its destined home.

We moved in on a gloomy November day in 1935. Apart from working equipment we had no furniture and searched the second-hand shops for tables, chairs and book shelves for the elegant front part which we painted pale grey, and hung long green curtains off a film set at the tall windows. The whole effect was strangely austere and formal, but it was a quiet and cool refuge from the area beyond the pillars under the domed roof which was very hot in summer and in winter freezing, with rain dripping relentlessly into bowls and buckets ranged round the working space.

Yet another hazard was the family of fecund mice which invaded the Studio from the pub next door and swarmed under our feet. Both Buntie and I – though not our intrepid colleague Connie – were terrified of mice and attempted to evade them by arranging chairs on which – we thought – we could move about the Studio. But a brief experiment proved that neither of us had a head for heights and there would have to be some other solution, for meanwhile the mice were multiplying. So it was decided that the best solution would be a cat, and somehow we acquired Phoebe, an enchanting Persian kitten. The effect was instantaneous, and thankfully we settled down and left it all to her. But, alas, not for long, for Phoebe began to show more interest in the cacophony of tom cats ranged daily along the garden wall than in the mice under her feet. So, broken-hearted, we had to let her go, and reluctantly submitted to the very last resort – the ruthlessly effective 'Rodent Operative.'

Although Studio E was a place for working but not for living in, and from every point of view it was a blessing that we were all able to get away to the bosom of our families each evening – unless we were working overnight which was not unusual.

It must be admitted that the work produced by Creative Arts was almost entirely frivolous, concerned as it was with promoting the interests of large organizations such as J. Lyons with their elaborate window displays, the Music Corporation of America which demanded lavish settings for their spectacular cabarets at Grosvenor House, and exhibition stands advertising expensive products to be shown at Trade Fairs at Olympia and Earls Court and in the provinces. Nevertheless, what all this activity lacked in seriousness was made up for by ingenuity, imagination, and hard work.

As well as these bread-and-butter jobs there were also the films for which Buntie was art director at one or other of the film studios. She would work out ideas at Studio E and develop them on the actual sets, often at night when the studios would be free of personnel. These were films for which Jim, her half-brother, was director. He was a large and expansive man whose popularity with the technicians, as well as Buntie's own gift for making happy relationships

7

with people doing a job, forestalled resentment at working under the direction of a young woman, and needless to say it was not long before she earned their respect and affection. Her great friend was Alf, the Master Carpenter. She was devoted to him and he watched over her like a benevolent uncle.

*

Her brother Jim, whose full name was James Elder Wills, was the son of Buntie's mother – who came of a theatrical family – by her first husband. After his father died, she married Henry Langmead and their first child was christened Phyllis Christine, but because she was born on the first night of a play called *Buntie Pulls the Strings*, in which a member of the family was playing, she became known as Buntie.

Jim was in his teens by the time Buntie was born and her sister Jennie did not appear till eight years later, so Buntie led an isolated childhood. According to early snapshots she was a beguiling child with a freckled face, a mop of curly dark hair and the quizzical blue-green eyes which were to intrigue so many admirers later on. She had few if any friends at that time and created her own interests, which involved spending hours alone in the woods behind the family home in Golders Green. Even as a child she was passionately independent and resented any attempt to treat her as an inferior on account of her lack of years.

Their mother was Scottish, a large and beautiful woman with a kind and tranquil manner which belied a strong will and the same implacable quality which Buntie sometimes displayed There was a close bond between them and a shared sense of the ridiculous. I recall on one occasion coming across these two lovely women slowly strolling along the street arm-in-arm, heads together, absorbed in a laughing tête-a-tête which, while excluding those around them, created an impression of irresistible charm. When in 1946 her mother died after a painful illness, Buntie, as always keeping her deepest feelings to herself, went to Cornwall and stayed alone in a caravan until she felt able to face the world again.

Jim was an architect and artist and a dominating personality. He was twelve years Buntie's senior and her idol and it was largely his influence which was the incentive for her to choose art as her career in the first place. She talked constantly about him and for much of her youth he was her reference point in most things. When she went to work with him at the film studios, it was inevitably assumed that her surname was the same as his so to all intents and purposes she became Buntie Wills. This suited her very well for she thoroughly disliked her baptismal names, but because Phyllis was how she was known at art school it was many years before any of us could bring ourselves to call her Buntie.

During the war Jim, who had an ingenious mind, was a Lieutenant Colonel with a cover-up title as 'Director of Camouflage'; he devised particularly devilish booby-traps such as dead rats filled with high explosives for the benefit of any enemy troops who came across them. A 'ghosted' paperback called *Camouflage* relates his diverse operations in many theatres of war, and includes a photograph of his large and imposing figure on the steps of his headquarters, the Victoria and Albert Museum, awaiting a visit from King George VI.

*

In 1938 when war with Germany appeared to be imminent and conscription for women as well as men seemed likely, Buntie and I, finding it laughable to imagine ourselves dragooned into the Women's Services and wearing uniform, decided that the best course would be to join the Women's Land Army, which appeared to offer useful war work and perhaps a kind of freedom. Almost immediately we were posted to the home farm of a landed estate in the West Country for two weeks training. There we overlapped for one week, and while I was cleaning out pig-sties I could hear Buntie, always fearful of large animals, in the distance bawling at the cows she was vainly trying to persuade into a field from which a frisky horse was intent on getting out. And while she was having a restful time pruning peaches in the kitchen garden, I wa trying to squeeze some milk out of a reluctant cow while perched on a two-legged stool – the cowman's little joke! We were lodged with the families of 'upper' servants, Buntie with the chauffeur and I with the butler. We actually did meet at the Manor House where we were bidden for afternoon tea, and were fascinated by the untrammelled eating habits of the aristocracy.

This experience, however, became irrelevant when war was declared in September 1939, for we were both immediately sent off to a farm in Kent where we worked in the hop gardens, apple orchards, and potato fields of a 'gentleman farmer.' Up at six every morning we were driven after breakfast to our daily venue, worked till five-thirty, and were then driven back to the house where we dined formally with the family. Idyllic as it may sound, the work was gruelling, though it was lightened by the droves of East Enders who turned up for their annual hop-picking holiday, and by the equally unrestrained village women who were part of the regular work force. Between them our whole experience as well as our vocabularies were greatly enriched.

Some time in November this episode came to an abrupt end when all the Land-girls – there were several of us – were perfunctorily informed by the farmer that the work was now completed and our labour no longer required: we could however return in the spring if we so wished. This unforeseen situation had to be reported to the Women's Land Army headquarters, who then decided that we were appropriate candidates for the Forestry Service which, we were gratified to learn, was reserved for the 'cream' of the Land Army.

Again we were sent for 'training,' this time to the Forest of Dean as potential forestry measurers with a group of about twenty-five women from diverse backgrounds and professions, to a college for young men forestry students who had all, except the shy one who had to take charge of us, been called up. We slept in a bleak dormitory where we washed in cold water in a communal basin, and had meals consisting of bread and tea and tinned tomatoes at long trestle-tables. On this diet we set out every morning at six-thirty in deep snow (the winters of 1940 and 1941 were the coldest for many years) to trudge miles into the Forest in order to learn about trees in their habitat. There is a somewhat unflattering snapshot included in the photograph section, of Buntie and the rest of us warming our frozen hands at a bonfire in the forest during a lunch break, a motley crew, all attired in our personal versions of the inadequate Land Army uniforms. Sometimes there were sessions at the College, conducted by an embarrassed elderly gentleman who had to lecture to us on arboricultural subjects, which turned out quite irrelevant to the work we were soon to be engaged in.

On the first evening a reception had been arranged for us all to meet and fraternize over drinks and sandwiches, but while the rest of us were mingling and talking, one individual had taken herself to the other end of the dining hall and was spread-eagled over a long table on which was an enormous map. Buntie – who else? – went over and asked what on earth she was doing, and was grudgingly informed that this was part of a Town Planning thesis and that she was Jacqueline Tyrwhitt. There was nothing to suggest at the time that this unusual individual was to become a catalyst in Buntie's future and in mine.

11

After four weeks of so-called training we were all dispersed to various forests throughout the country belonging to the Forestry Commission. Several of us, including Buntie and me and some of the friends we had made at the College, were sent to the New Forest where each was appointed to a small sawmill. Accommodation had been requisitioned for us in the surrounding villages where we found we were much resented by our landladies, which is hardly surprising. This discomfiting situation as well as the difficulty of getting to our widely dispersed sawmills – usually on foot, for deep snow in the Forest made cycling impossible for many weeks – encouraged some of us to search for more accessible lodgings.

For Buntie and me and another girl called Irena this awkward period did not last long, for a sawyer at my mill told me that a farm nearby where he daily went to get milk, had rooms to let. These turned out to be in an annexe adjoining the farmhouse which would accommodate all of us comfortably. What with the additional luxuries of constant hot water and fresh farm produce and all for a sum we could just manage out of our wages of thirty shillings a week, we considered ourselves blessed. Getting to work was now straightforward; Buntie and Irena could drive to their sawmills in Irena's dilapidated Austin 7, and I could walk across the fields to mine. But if Irena happened to be away, Buntie would have to cycle. She was quite unrelated to machinery and her attitude to bicycles was haphazard. Somehow she would manage to get on and keep going but could never master getting off, and would simply find a convenient hedge and fall into it. Hilarious though this was to others, laughter was not encouraged.

For our less fortunate friends from other parts of the Forest, the cottage became a gathering point where there was freedom to talk about the war and about ourselves and our problems concerning the work we were having to undertake with so little preparation.

The purpose of our jobs as forestry measurers was to supervise and record the input of timber and the corresponding output of railway-sleepers and pit props, all of which had to be checked for dimensions and condition. Our expertise was minimal and we had to use considerable tact with the experts we were supposed to supervise, not always successfully for they naturally resented these ignorant female intruders In general we each achieved a mutual tolerance and a *modus vivendi*, sometimes through one of the sawyers who would take a liking to an individual measurer. For me this would mean being invited on a particularly freezing day to join the sawmill's crew on the seats behind the engine which belched out suffocating smoke, to eat my sandwiches and sup cold tea from a bottle passed from hand to hand. This could be classed as a test of mutual toleration and becoming one of the team.

Apart from such occasional shelter, we spent the whole of the first year with no protection from the extremes of weather typical of that period of the war. In the following year we were provided with unheated huts as offices where we had to keep our records, and later still fearsome stoves appeared which had to be fed constantly with green wood, puffing out the same stifling smoke as did the engine, which made the huts almost uninhabitable and the cold outside preferable.

The first severe winter was succeeded by a perfect spring when the idea of war seemed utterly remote. But then followed the idyllic summer of 1940, when war itself became a reality and the Battle of Britain coruscated above our heads and fighter planes spiralled out of a brilliant sky. German bombers returning from devastating the Midland cities, released their remaining bombs indiscriminately on farm land and forest, and during daylight their fighter planes flew up and down the streets of the surrounding small towns, killing or wounding many of the inhabitants.

Tucked away in our secluded farm-house, we became conditioned to ignoring the boom of enemy planes passing overhead on their nightly bombing expeditions to the Midland cities, until – one pitch dark night – a tremendous explosion shook us all out of our beds. Asked by the sisters who owned the farm to go with them to see if the cows were safe we groped our way across the fields, coming across no dead or wounded cows but a large dark patch on the grass which could only be a bomb crater. Standing round the edge we peered down into the deeper darkness; it revealed nothing, so with sighs of relief we trooped back to bed and to sleep. But not for long. In the early hours of the morning we were again flung out of our beds by an even more shattering explosion. Realizing it must have been a time-bomb we'd been standing over we did not venture out again till daylight when it was possible to see the extent of the damage; an enormous crater extending over several fields and filled with severed trees. It was only by the Grace of God that the bomb had fallen on a slope away from the house, so that it was still standing and all its occupants still alive.

In London later in the year, the Blitz was at its height, and necessary visits there entailed interminable journeys in darkened trains which crept past blacked-out towns as we crammed the corridors among exhausted troops. Buntie was often among them for, war or no war, she still took on design projects as they came along, such as a scheme for a directors' dining room in the City and murals for a nightclub in Soho. Until many years later, when she came to a painful turning point during her training as a psychotherapist, she never turned down the challenge of any new design work, perhaps with her post-war occupation in mind. A card among her papers with a scribbled note– 'Gone to London – sausages in oven' – proved that she was also playing her part in the domestic scene. I recall that on winter mornings she would get up early to make sure that we all started the day with a large bowl of porridge 'to keep us warm inside,' as recommended by her much-loved Scottish mother.

It was almost certainly on one of these journeys that Buntie, standing in the corridor of a train packed with Troops, was chatted up by a young man, not in uniform, who told her he was on three months leave from his job in the Colonial Service in Nigeria. By the time the train had crept through the black-out to Waterloo he was madly in love with her and chased her for the rest of his leave – without avail. On his return to Nigeria he confided the story of his broken heart to the wife of a colleague. This wife was Maggie, whom Buntie had helped to decorate her brother's rugger club. Although he never told her the girl's name, by piecing together little details she came to realize the girl was 'Phyllis Langmead' – a 'coincidence' that was a mark of Buntie's distinctiveness.

While most of our colleagues were living in villages around the Forest and we three shared the cottage, Jacqueline Tyrwhitt had, true to form, found herself a caravan where in her spare time she could pursue her town planning studies undisturbed and also carry out surveys of the surrounding countryside as a practical exercise. This useful and harmless occupation led to her being arrested and interrogated by the police, suspicious local inhabitants having watched her activities and reported them. That afternoon we had all been invited to a garden party given for us by local ladies, and everything hung in the air while we awaited the missing measurer. The crest-fallen figure who eventually appeared apologized but did not explain her late arrival. Later she told us that after an intense grilling she had been released with a severe warning against incurring further suspicion and wasting their time. Typically, she considered the whole thing ridiculous and was furious at being deprived of her surveying practice.

15

Occasionally Jacky would turn up at the cottage on her own, perhaps as light relief from her planning studies. She was an intense character concerned always with 'The Job,' whatever it might be, rather than with personal relationships – or so it appeared. Although she must have considered the work Buntie and I had been doing before the war quite nugatory, she revelled in Buntie's gift of humour, which could throw an amusing light on matters which Jacky herself would take seriously, and her stern but beautiful face would break into delighted laughter.

On one such occasion in 1941, Jacky told us that she had been invited by the Director of the London School of Planning for Regional Development, A.A. Rowse, to take over his job when he was called up for military service. At first she declined because she regarded her war work as more important, but under pressure and with great reluctance, she finally agreed and was exempted from the Forestry Service on the grounds that she was not only releasing a man for military service but was also taking his place in the realm of post-war planning.

Several months after her departure Jacky suddenly appeared at the farm with a surprising proposal: that Buntie and I should both join her at the Association for Planning and Regional Reconstruction, as the former L.S.P.R.D. had become, where she considered our pre-war skills would be useful in the preparation of maps and plans for publication, a proposal that was to change the whole direction of Buntie's life, and mine. At the time Buntie was doubtful, perhaps because she did not see herself as part of a large organization and needed time for reflection, but for reasons of my own I grasped at the opportunity to return to London, and early in 1942 it was my turn to be released from the Forestry Service. Several months later Buntie decided also to make the move. Even now I can recall Jacky's delight and relief that this versatile character would at last become a member of the team and with her gaiety and humour lighten the heavy academic atmosphere which prevailed there.

So, late in 1942, Buntie left the Forestry Service and returned to London. Her intention was to live in Studio E which we had retained for the duration of the war at a peppercorn rent. I had not wanted to live there – recalling the drawbacks – and had found myself a small flat in Hampstead. However when Buntie was actually there she realized that what with the glass roof not only leaking but vulnerable to bomb blasts, and with the inadequate heating and other disadvantages, she would do better to give up Studio E and take the vacant Studio H upstairs. At that time there was an old lady living in the two small rooms opposite and when later she died, Buntie was able to take them over.

Having been at the A.P.R.R. for several months before Buntie arrived there, I was conscious of the palpable change of atmosphere once she had settled in and had time to grasp the scope of her new job. Part of it was to be aware of what everyone else was doing and to get to know individuals, so she was in a position to smooth out tensions between the gifted people who were working there, most of them refugees from occupied Europe. This was just what Jacky had hoped for, since to her such personal differences were an absurd waste of time.

But it was Buntie's professional approach to whatever work she was engaged in that brought the two together in a creative partnership. The varied material produced by Jacky and the other people there was translated by Buntie over the years into a series of superb publications. She took over layout and design, dealt with technical experts and publishers and saw it all through the Press. By the time Jacky and she left in 1949-50, the Association had produced a body of material on every aspect of planning, which was to become invaluable to students as well as to all the professions engaged in postwar redevelopment.

17

From its beginning the Association had become a magnet which drew into its orbit people from many professions, and Buntie frequently attended discussions there on a variety of subjects: industrial relations, psychology, mental health and other relevant topics which interested her because they concerned human beings.

The chairman of the Association was Lord Forrester, later the Earl of Verulam, known to all as 'Jim'; he was impressed by Buntie's versatility and asked her, in addition to her regular work, to design an advertising campaign for Enfield Cable Works in which he was involved as an industrial executive. This entailed her going with him to the cable works, usually at night when the furnaces were at full blast, which gave her the opportunity to talk to the men working there and to get some idea of industrial relations in action while gathering material for the publicity campaign. On other nights she would be among the group of people who accompanied him to Lyons Corner House for cups of tea and discussions on current projects, while air-raids and later flying bombs wrought havoc and devastation around them.

Among the eminent people on the board of directors was Professor Eva Taylor of Birkbeck College who took a general interest in the work produced by the Association and consequently was in frequent contact with Buntie. It was she who suggested that Buntie should do a course in geography at Birkbeck in 1943-44. The large binder holding her course work is full of maps, diagrams, statistics and notes covering physical factors in the British Isles and the world at large, but no essays or other written material. The purpose of this study is not clear, but it may have been a challenge she could not resist because at school, according to her end-of-term reports, geography had been one of her most successful subjects.

In January 1944 Buntie contributed a pungent article to a journal called *World Review*, edited by Edward Hulton, entitled 'This is Planning.' The title was probably meant to be ironic, for in it she attacked government inertia with regard to the importance of post-war planning, and extolled the work of independent organisations such as the A.P.R.R. with its series of broadsheets, maps and other vital publications, as well as its correspondence courses especially written for would-be planners then in the Forces overseas, and later to develop into The School of Planning at Gordon Square. It could have been this article as well as Professor Taylor's recommendation which was instrumental in her being made a member of the Geographical Society in April 1944.

The A.P.R.R. spread itself over a five-storey building in Gordon Square. Jacky, Buntie and the administration were on the ground floor, Jacky lived in a flat at the top, and the floors in between housed researchers and map designers: I was one of these. In addition to her other gifts, Buntie was a brilliant cartoonist, and though never unkind would relentlessly point up the absurdities in other people – and in herself. When she thought Jacky too exacting she would put up witty caricatures of her on the notice board in the hall for all to see. Jacky would hastily remove them without a word, but when years later Buntie stayed with her in Greece, she produced them all out of a drawer and together they went through them, with mutual enjoyment. A very typical one was of Jacky, who never stopped working, starting up the stairs at the end of a busy day to her eyrie on the fifth floor, carrying an enormous tray piled high with books and papers, large rolls of maps under her arms – to begin her evening's work..

It was Jacky who, inadvertently, brought about a meeting between Buntie and an exceptional man who was to become of great significance to her. He was an eminent French philosopher who came to London soon after the end of the war, when travel from the Continent had again become possible, to take part in a weekend conference. Jacky was supposed to be responsible for his welfare but at the last moment had to be elsewhere, much to her chagrin, and grudgingly asked Buntie if she would look after him in her top-floor flat, impressing on her his eminence and importance. Buntie had had other plans and was incensed at being forced into such an obligation and having her weekend invaded by a stranger, however distinguished, but grudgingly complied.

Her encounter with this stranger was electrifying. Between them there was an immediate recognition and the knowledge that their meeting was predestined. They knew that in a previous life – during the French Revolution – they had been close companions who, among the panic-stricken throng running towards Notre Dame for sanctuary, had become separated. Buntie had reached the church just as the great doors were closing and was left outside, alone and desolate. Coming together again in this life they recognized in each other a level of intuition in which they could express their deepest feelings and insights in complete harmony. It was a genuinely romantic encounter of a kind which most human beings imagine and hope for but are seldom privileged to experience.

It is known that they met again in Paris several times and visited galleries together and that they wrote to each other for several years with the same warmth and understanding, until suddenly his letters ceased. Buntie was desolated for she knew he must have died, and with him the outward expression of their unique and enduring affinity.

Both Buntie and Jacky were exceptional individuals and curiously alike, in that each was dedicated to 'Work,' although their motivations were not the same. Jacky had once implied that the work which occupied her whole life was compensation for some other lack. For Buntie all work was motivated by the necessity to be independent and to use all her talents to the full. They both led dedicated and fruitful lives, Buntie ultimately concerned with the individual's inner needs, Jacky with the environmental needs of human beings all over the world. She travelled widely, meeting illustrious and influential people who valued and spread her ideas – she referred to herself as a catalyst – until in 1964 she settled near Athens in her own specially designed house and among kindred spirits where she cultivated a garden of her own, always her dearest ambition. On two occasions Buntie stayed with her there. Jacky became editor of *Ekistics*, a Greek journal concerned with human settlements, and when she died in 1983 a whole edition was dedicated to her. She once said to Buntie, 'I am a "thing" person, and you are a "people" person.' She did herself an injustice, for in an impersonal way she was kind and generous and opened doors for many people. She was also perceptive about Buntie who, once she had embarked on her profession as a psychotherapist, made people – individuals – her preoccupation until the end of her life.

*

In a curious way Buntie's true calling emerged through the death of her father. Although she had never been close to him, his death in 1943 stirred her deepest feelings, for it became her responsibility to clear up his private and business affairs and through this she was forced to recognize how much she had meant to him and how little she had known him. Sometime later the period of stress she went through after this harrowing experience as well as exhaustion caused by overwork culminated in a strange physical aberration which occurred one evening when she was visiting my mother, as she did quite often: they were good friends and had interests in common. Later my mother told me that suddenly, while they were talking, Buntie fell asleep in the middle of a sentence and slept deeply until my mother, knowing Buntie had to get back to Cunningham Place in the black-out, woke her. In getting out of her chair, Buntie discovered her left arm to be paralyzed and it did not respond to attempts to revive it. After consulting doctor and specialists and submitting to a variety of treatments including strong electrical charges and green pills, none of which had

21

any effect, she was told that unless she followed a very strict regime for the rest of her life, it would develop into complete paralysis of the whole of her left side. Having heard this dire news she went home to try to assimilate what she had been told. She sat down and became very quiet and thought about all that had led up to her father's death. After this she felt better, threw the large box of green pills into the dustbin and went to bed, deciding to consider the whole situation the following day. The next morning her arm was completely normal.

Buntie realized that something very strange had been going on and that she must somehow uncover the mystery. At that time she knew nothing about psychology, but when later she came across *Modern Man in Search of a Soul* by Carl Gustav Jung, it marked the beginning of her own search. She began by reading widely, in particular the works of Carl Jung in which she found great personal satisfaction. She attended lectures, discovered the Guild of Pastoral Psychology and became a member.

In the summer of 1946 Buntie was in a train on her way to the country for a weekend with friends. She was reading, yet again, *Modern Man in Search of a Soul*. This time it seemed to be saying something personal to her about her own need for psychotherapy. The train stopped at a station. On impulse she got out, found a telephone, looked up the number of Philip Metman, a well-known psychotherapist she had heard lecture at the Guild of Pastoral Psychology a few weeks earlier, and rang his number. He answered. She tried to explain. He said, 'Take the next train back and come here. I shall be waiting for you.' So began her first plunge into the private world of her own psyche, a Jungian analysis which went on for three years. (Later Philip Metman was to recommend her for further training analysis with Mrs. Toni Sussman, 'since she has the qualities and abilities which will make her a psychotherapist of high standard.')

It was during this period that Buntie began to realize where her true interests and the future direction of her work lay. It happened that she met a healer who needed somewhere to carry on his work in the evenings and, typically, offered him the use of the room which later became her consulting room. Occasionally she sat in on his sessions and watched him at work with the people who came to him, and in doing so learned a lot about them. When, suddenly, he died, these simple and bereft people were left in a vacuum. She felt she could not leave them stranded and without help and offered to see them herself for the time being. Some of them accepted, and these became the nucleus of her eventual practice. I remember her saying that as time went by, the more her experience grew and developed, the more intellectually demanding her patients became.

In the meantime Buntie was finding her job at the A.P.R.R. increasingly onerous, for Jacky was frequently away, attending conferences all over the world on various aspects of planning, and leaving her to deal with the day-to-day running of the organization as well as her own work there. So it was not surprising, considering all the developments in her personal life, that in December 1948 she wrote to Lord Forrester saying that she would like to resign from the full-time staff as from the following March 31. She wrote, 'My sympathies and beliefs don't rest with the planning world and become less so as time goes on. This incompatibility is an ever increasing strain to me.' She goes on to say however that after the end of the following April she would be free to act as part-time consultant and adviser on presentation if he so wished. This offer was accepted and she stayed on there, very productively, until some time in 1950 when Lord Forrester suddenly died and the A.P.R.R. ceased to exist.

Buntie's reason for not taking up her consultation work till the following year was that in the spring of 1949 she was in Paris designing decor and costumes for a ballet company, La Compagnie de Cygne, in collaboration with her friend Yanka

23

Zlatin. In the following August she agreed to collaborate with a firm of architects, on a part-time basis, on projects for the Festival of Britain which was to open in May 1951.

So it happened that Buntie and I left the A.P.R.R. at about the same time to go our separate ways, I eventually to be swallowed up in the vast environs of the London County Council and in the course of time to qualify as a town planner, Buntie to settle down at Cunningham Place and resume for the time being her 'creative arts' persona and take on all the design work that was coming her way. At the same time she was absorbed in her Jungian studies as well as seeing people in need of help.

Perhaps it was these preoccupations, as well as the same intuition which had caused her to break a journey in order to see Philip Metman three years previously, which took her to a weekend conference on some aspect of Jungian psychotherapy in Birmingham in the summer of 1950. The weather was very hot, the conference hall stifling and the talk tedious, so, Buntie told me later, she left to find somewhere cool and green where she could be alone. Walking through the corridors looking for a way out she became aware of footsteps and a tapping behind her, and glancing around saw a tiny figure with a stick. She walked faster. The footsteps followed. At last out in the open she saw a gate into a street through which she thought she could escape. It was locked. The footsteps caught up with her. With a beaming smile and a strong continental accent her pursuer said, 'You are running away?' Offended, Buntie said, 'I am looking for a tree.' The tiny old lady replied, 'So am I. Let us go and find one together.' There was no escape. So Buntie and Mrs. Toni Sussman, psychoanalyst and pupil of Carl Jung, walked the scorching streets of Birmingham together and found a tree. There and back and under the tree they talked, and Buntie understood why she had come to Birmingham. On her return she gave me a very funny account of what turned out later to be a crucial point in her future career.

In the following February, Mrs. Sussman sent a note to Buntie saying that it would be nice to meet again and suggesting a date and time. That it was she who renewed the contact between them could have been because during their long conversation under the tree in Birmingham, she had intuitively recognised Buntie as a true psychotherapist. In one of her talks in the 'Toni book,' which Buntie helped edit and publish after Toni's death, she says, 'Psychology is not only a science, it is also an art, an art which makes use of the methods of science. An artist must be born. In the same way you never become a psychotherapist – you are one by birth. It is a gift. Only then can you take up the study of this subject...'. And having realized the joy of finding such a gift to nurture and develop, she suggested this meeting. Whatever transpired then, in the following September Mrs. Sussman accepted Buntie as a pupil on the recommendation of her previous analyst, Philip Metman. At the same time she insisted that Buntie should undertake a course in psychology at the Newman Association, a London University extension course. This consisted of twenty-four lectures between November 1951 and April 1952, which required written comments. These lectures and Buntie's replies are in her files. Her replies to some penetrating questions and her tutor's responses reveal that stimulating arguments were carried on between them during those few months.

Buntie's work with Mrs. Sussman entailed continual self-exploration which she wrote down as homework. In one of these papers in 1953 she writes about an experience in the spring of 1952 which was for her 'the turning point.' She says,

'It is possible that the real turning point was when I met you in Birmingham and we went for that walk. Certainly I was aware of a meeting then that was part of "the other thread." But the switch-over came last year during a night of sleepless agony. Briefly – having successfully designed and carried out some display work, I was in the middle of carrying out a second commission. Nothing came. All my creative energy seemed to be drained off elsewhere. There had been struggles before at odd periods but somehow I had always managed to escape defeat and produce the baby.

'This time – dimly – I knew it had got to be sacrificed, that I had to renounce my only asset and all that went with it, including the prides: the pride of knowing my job, the pride of never letting anyone down, the pride of accumulated knowledge, the pride of producing the answer to a problem, the pride of past successes and reputation. The "Hound of Heaven" had caught up with me at last. That may sound dramatic, but those feet had become louder and increasingly relentless over the previous months. I faced complete failure in all I had felt most security in. I fought hard and doggedly and refused to accept this ultimatum. It was no good – I could not do a thing beyond drawing a swan. It was the only thing that, scribbling down ideas, kept cropping up. It had no bearing on the job at all. The words, "swan song," kept repeating themselves in my head. Gabrielle witnessed this whole struggle and stayed by me all night. [She had telephoned urgently and asked me to go over.] It was she who said suddenly, "Why not give up the whole thing?" With relief, I understood in a flash what had been sensed but not acknowledged I admitted complete defeat and surrendered. All my burdens were lifted and I knew that here was a new beginning. For the first time I felt part of a whole. It was not for me to decide anything any more but only to obey.

'In spite of many ups and downs, shortcomings and backslidings that have happened since, I have found the inner security that only comes when one stops placing one's trust in oneself and in other fallible human beings, and places it in God. The need to please and impress people is a need for consolation and reward that is false and trivial, a waste of time and energy. It is unworthy. Worse, it is a world of complete illusion. My new job in life which till this time I had only grasped with one hand and not with the other which had been busy clinging on to the past, comes to me as it should. I mean, here, not through my own self-determined efforts. I know that now I have a function that unless it is fulfilled in the right way and from the source will be taken away. I am grateful beyond words for the opportunity and for the Teacher to whom I have been sent. I hope one day to be able to carry out her teaching.

'This is a pretty bold statement but the "realization" that came to me differed very little from the many hundreds of accounts that have been written and expressed so beautifully by mystics and poets all over the world. A further and fully illuminating "realization" (not experience) came later when I was listening to Avekananda. It very nearly broke me into fragments it was so unexpected and so powerful. The Word was right there in the room. I could not be articulate about it, no expression could possibly be adequate . . . .

'Writing this produced a dream which seems relevant so I am putting it down:

'I am introduced to the Original Bible. Note: I had been out to Mowbrays to buy a Bible for Gabrielle's birthday last week.

'I was with my father. There were several Bibles on a table. He said, "I want to introduce you to . . ." mentioning the name of a young priest, "and for you to go through this carefully with him," pointing to one of the Bibles. I said, "Is that the one I found?" and he answered very firmly, "No, the one I found" It was a very large volume and extremely old. Important: I put on a hat (a thing I never wear) out of reverence for the occasion. We went into a kind of library where many people were sitting at desks poring over books they had lifted from the many shelves. A strange young man leant against a bookcase in the background. I at once recognized him as someone I had met some time ago. My father introduced me as "Miss Wills." We took the Bible to a desk and sat down side by side. To my amazement when it was opened I realized it

27

was the Original Bible. It was entirely written by hand on papyrus and was illustrated on every page with exquisite colour drawings. The title page said *The A ... Bible.* I couldn't remember the name when I awoke but I asked E who said there was a Bible called *The Adenoye Bible.* I have never heard of this. The young man started to turn over the pages and explain many things to me.'

After that soul-searching night Buntie abandoned all connection with the commercial world, but continued to make the most of her wide experience as artist and designer by encouraging others in whatever creative expression was their own. She opened doors for many people, as I have heard from several of my friends who went to her as a therapist. And Catherine Yarrow has written in the introduction to her exhibition in 1988 that it was not until she met Buntie that she came into the full flowering of her gifts as an artist.

For herself, while carrying on her own practice at Cunningham Place, Buntie concentrated on her analysis with Toni Sussman, who invited her to join the Monday Group meetings, held at her home in Gloucester Place, which she had begun in Berlin and continued when she came to England in 1937. At these meetings, Mrs. Sussman, who was herself a Catholic, spoke about the various sources of religious belief and the many forms of meditation, in particular those which had originated in the Indian Continent. As I discovered when later, through Buntie, I went to her for help with my own problems and later still was admitted to the Monday Group, Mrs. Sussman radiated a quality of great inner strength controlled by spiritual discipline; her teaching was incisive and illuminating.

My personal experience of Mrs. Sussman was more down to earth. The warm expansive smile and outstretched hands which first greeted me concealed a stern and objective intelligence which left me no illusions about myself. As a therapist she sat and watched, listening intently, and by saying little drew out all I was most reluctant to reveal. Her usual comment on my personal revelations was a disconcerting, 'I – I –I,' which spoke volumes about my ego. So it was a surprise to me when she suggested that I too should join the prestigious Monday Group. Accepting her invitation with apprehension, I attended the group for some time, attempting to absorb her teaching on the various forms of meditation and taking copious notes. The private sessions drew out extraordinary dreams, significant and sometimes overwhelming, whose meaning I had to grapple with while she watched and listened, almost in silence. The time came when changes in my life made it difficult for me to go regularly to see her, or to the group, though I still sometimes sought her advice. Later she moved to Brighton to be with her daughter, where Buntie visited her several times until her death in 1967.

Buntie's professional training with Mrs. Sussman went on until 1955 when she applied to Dr. C.A. Meier of the Jung Institute at Zurich for permission to study Professor Jung's seminars under Mrs. Sussman's guidance. At about the same time she was passed as a Jungian psychotherapist by Dr. Graham Howe and Mrs. Sussman, and gave a lecture entitled, 'What is Resistance?' (based on the paralyzed arm) at the Open Way Clinic in February of the same year.

In December 1956 Buntie received the following letter from Mrs. Sussman, which was to bring about unforeseen changes in her working life. It said:

'My dear Buntie,

'In case I have to leave you in one way or another could you please take on our Group? This thought: you – Buntie – will carry on what started in June 1937 – would be great joy for me and surely for all the others.

'You will not be without me or my spirit – never.

'My blessing and love as always.

Yours, Toni'

29

This letter caused in Buntie, so she told me, a turmoil of conflicting emotions: gratitude for Toni's trust in her; dismay at the idea of taking on more responsibility; uncertainty about the underlying feelings of the group, several of whom had been with Toni since its beginning in 1937; but above all, doubt about her own spiritual fitness for such a role.

At that time Buntie was happy with her own life as it was. She had been through strenuous years since the war, working hard, taking much responsibility, studying widely before and after meeting Toni and learning from her, and had settled down to using all this for the benefit of others. And, at last, she had some time for all her personal interests. But Toni was perhaps the only living individual for whom Buntie felt reverence as well as deep personal love. Through knowing and learning from this unique human being, her own life had been transformed. So whatever her own doubts, there could be only one answer to Toni's request. It simply became a question of rearranging her life and stretching time and energy to encompass this new challenge. Once this decision was clear in her mind, she wrote to Mrs. Sussman:

'Dearest Toni,

'It is with the deepest part of myself that I say 'yes' to you – as always – in this case sustained in the acceptance of great responsibility by your spirit, blessings and love. I understand completely when you confirmed at the last Monday Group that we are one organism. I will serve it at any time that you may have to leave us, to the best of my capacity in Spirit and in Truth according to your teaching and under your guidance.

'I thank you for the confidence and trust you have placed in me.

'Your ever loving pupil,

Buntie'

It was not until October 1957 that Mrs. Sussman finally gave up her Monday Group and Buntie arranged for it to be held in the cramped space of her waiting room at Cunningham Place. At that time it consisted of several members of Toni's own group who later were joined by others whom Buntie knew would add strength and make their own contribution.

For the first two years Buntie carried on Toni's teachings in her own way, based mainly on what she had learned about them from the multifarious aspects of Indian philosophy, mysticism, and Jungian psychology. In 1959 she asked Helah Fox to join with her in a change of approach, introducing the esoteric teachings of the Qabalah, the Tree of Life, which Helah had studied in depth for many years. For the following twelve years Buntie used the Tree of Life as a background to psychological studies, until in 1971 the Group came to a natural end. This group must have been very different from its predecessor in the way talks were presented, for while Mrs. Sussman always spoke spontaneously from her great store of knowledge, Buntie's talks were carefully researched and prepared and can still be studied.

*

In 1971 Buntie was able once again to get possession of Studio E, twenty-eight years after she and I had left it at the outbreak of war. (After the end of the war several well-known painters had rented it for various periods, among them Matthew Smith whose portrait of Buntie used to hang in her own room and now is with her sister Jennie.) For Buntie, it was a great joy to be able to make Studio E a part of her working life again.

The next few years were a fruitful time for her and the people in her life. Inevitably Studio E became a meeting place where groups were formed for new activities – psychodrama, meditation, poetry readings, T'ai-Chi Ch'uan, and gatherings where talks were given and films shown. In the

31

course of time Studio E became adorned with the artistic creations of those whose talents Buntie had fostered and encouraged, as well as those of friends – painters, potters, lithographers – many of them professional artists. And, because she loved children of all ages, she sometimes became involved with those she had known from birth and who grew up visiting Studio E with their parents. Buntie encouraged them to draw and paint and write and, as their great friend, would now and then become one of them, and they would all paint together, side by side. Many of their creations occupied a place of their own on the the Studio mantelpiece.

*

In her role as a psychotherapist, Buntie was not always to be found in Studio E or her consulting room at Cunningham Place. Quite a lot of her spare time was spent making lengthy journeys to the outer purlieus of London and beyond, visiting people cooped up in hospitals and nursing homes, bringing hope and solace and even, sometimes, bringing the patient away with her. In emergencies nearer home, she would drop everything and be there with remedies and flowers and sometimes specialist help and, as a true Libran, make everything comfortable – rearrange pillows, light several candles and create a soothing ambience to give the impression that being ill was an experience to make the most of.

Distance was no object to her when someone she cared about was in need of help. There was the occasion when, one bitter winter, she accompanied a close friend, a Roman Catholic who was mortally ill, on a journey to Lourdes. The incidents of the journey as she related them to me later made clear that it was a true pilgrimage, each phase of it presenting unexpected hazards which had to be overcome, some of them quite bizarre.

On another occasion, one of Buntie's inspired journeys led to a significant and lasting friendship. As it happened, she and I were spending a weekend with mutual friends at Ewhurst in Surrey. On the Sunday morning Buntie announced – much to everyone's amazement – that she had to go that day to visit someone in hospital at Midhurst, a man she had never met but whom she had heard was in need of help. Brushing aside all protests and warnings about the lack of cross-country transport on Sundays, she set off into the blue, assuring us that she would get there somehow. Of course she did, and arriving at the hospital discovered Robert Smith and – as he recounted at Buntie's memorial service – changed the direction of his life.

Recently I heard from Margaret Sankey that Buntie once told her how she always kept a large fund of bank notes hidden among books in case she was suddenly needed, and one night had used the whole of her reserves to go by taxi to the South Coast to deal with an emergency concerning one of her patients. Some of this hoard came to light after her death and led to puzzled speculation. Now all is revealed: for people, no limits on time or taxis.

Sometimes individuals dropped into Buntie's life apparently by chance and, though not concerned with her work or her other interests, turned out to have a particular significance for her. As she herself had written, 'It is the quality and experience of the other person that attracts me and that I want to be in touch with no matter what it is,' so these were mostly people who worked for a living: shop assistants, workmen, road sweepers, taxi drivers, someone waiting at a bus stop or whom she met in a train. Whoever they were, some alchemy drew them towards her, for a few minutes, a few hours or even for years.

Taxi drivers in particular had a special rapport with her, perhaps because both had solitary jobs which depended largely on strangers appearing out of the blue, and in the impersonal confines of a taxi-cab with a small window open between them they could establish a contact with no obligations attached. But, sometimes, the contact went further. There was the occasion, so delightfully related by Robert Smith at the memorial service, when Buntie called a taxi to take her to Regents Park because she felt the need to sit under a tree, the same impulse which had drawn her and Toni Sussman together some years earlier. On the way there she and the taxi driver talked, and went on talking under a spreading chestnut tree until it was time for her to return to Cunningham Place, both enriched by their mutual exchanges.

Often, when Buntie was coming to a meal with me, I would hear a taxi chugging away outside the house and would take the food out of the oven – and wait. Invariably it would be cold by the time she arrived at the top of the stairs, full of apologies but immersed in the confidences which had thrown a new light on the precarious lives of taxi drivers and quite indifferent to the dinner being cold. In time I learned it was better to leave it in the oven.

Bus stops too offered opportunities for fruitful communication which Robert Smith also spoke of when he referred to Buntie missing a bus and while waiting for the next had brought solace and hope to another traveller who had been contemplating suicide. On another occasion when some mission had taken her to East Anglia, she had fallen into conversation at a bus stop with a young couple who confided to her that they were in some domestic trouble, and so deep did the discussion go that it ended in her spending the night at their home and helping them to resolve the problem. I believe they were in friendly contact with each other for many years afterwards.

*

As a pupil of Toni Sussman, Buntie was familiar with the many forms of meditation, and during the summer of 1977 went to the Manjushri Institute near Ulverston in Cumbria to experience for herself meditation guided by a Tibetan Lama. For three weeks she willingly accepted the most basic physical comforts, for this centre had only recently been started and conditions were somewhat primitive, but the hours of sitting cross-legged on a cushion, as well as the back-breaking work in the grounds, she regarded as a privilege, a kind of sequel to her deep concern for Tibet and its occupation by an alien culture. The simplicity and order of daily life at the Institute and the long periods of meditation were for her the kind of freedom she had gone there to find. Although she tried to keep her profession secret, she could not disguise the magnetism which invariably drew people towards her, and it was seldom that she was able to fulfil her real need to be alone; that always, it seemed, had to take second place to the problems of others. But she told me how greatly she valued all the people she had come to know there and how much she had received from them.

In July 1982 Buntie embarked on yet another meditation experience, this time somewhere in Wiltshire. I drove her there on my way to Devon and wondered how she would cope with what appeared to be very basic conditions. However, so she told me later, she was treated with great consideration and given a tiny room to herself. She made the most of the opportunity to experience for ten days a new approach to meditation and the chance to take part in the discussions that followed, and enjoyed being with new and congenial people who very soon ceased to be strangers.

*

All the people who were close to Buntie must have been aware that beneath the patina of wit and humour which she presented to the world was a deeply serious individual. I first became conscious of this apparent contradiction on our early sketching expeditions into the countryside, and later during walks along the Cornish cliffs. Space and the open air seemed to provide the atmosphere, or perhaps the privacy, in which she felt safe to express her thoughts and attitudes and feelings. At the time I found the contrast with her customary gaiety disconcerting. In those days I was far from serious and too immature to appreciate such earnestness, and I wished she would remain on the same amusing level which delighted and entertained everyone who knew her. Later on I became aware that the spontaneous humour was a facade which concealed her natural shyness and sensitivity, while it captivated and misled people into believing her to be completely at ease in the world: this was never the case. She was always most truly herself when involved in work, whatever that happened to be, or with close friends and even those she kept in separate pockets. Social groups were anathema to her and, however well she concealed it, a source of discomfort.

As she wrote in a piece of homework for Mrs. Sussman, 'In working with others on a job, there is a centre of contact already there, but in private life or social intercourse the majority appear to float about on a surface sea of trivialities which I find impossible. Inevitably I am forced to try and plunge deeper, to find a sincere and "felt" point of contact . . . merely intellectual conversations bore me and I feel just cut off and unable to participate . . . . Facades irritate me and tire me in people and in books, as my own facades tire and irritate me.'

This essential seriousness and depth of feeling was apparent in the poetry she read when she was young. I remember how closely she identified with the Bronte sisters in their lonely manse on the Yorkshire Moors, particularly with Emily, whose austerity and toughness of spirit was an inspiration to her. 'No coward soul is mine,' she frequently read and talked about, and Emily's stoical defiance of death roused her respect and awe. With Francis Thomson she had a similar affinity, for his work expressed the same intensity of inner conflict which seemed to underlie her own nature. In her first homework for Mrs. Sussman, Buntie writes of the battles that went on within her between the many different selves she presents to others and says, 'I came across "The Hound of Heaven" this week and read it again and again with all the tremendous impact it had on me when in my early twenties. There is no escape from "all things betray thee who betrayest Me," so why does one go on running away? Where is there real humility in someone like me who constantly refuses to submit?'

Among the many other poets who aroused her interest at that time were William Blake, Gerard Manley Hopkins, Christina Rossetti, and Emily Dickinson, all introspective and original, qualities that Buntie admired. And T.S. Eliot, of course. There were others I cannot now recall, but after the war she became absorbed in the visionary poems of Edwin Muir, the Scottish writer whose work reflected his early sufferings and his quest to 'rediscover the drowned origins of the soul.' Later on, in the 1970s when the work of the renowned Russian poets, Osip Mandelstam, Nadezhda Akhmatova and their friend Marina Tsvetayeva, were published in English, works which had been savagely suppressed during the Stalin regime, Buntie became absorbed in their lives and the suffering that had been transmuted by them into such great poetry.

These fragmentary memories of the poetry which captured Buntie's imagination through the years suggest that she was interested mainly in verse which reflected the darker aspects of human life, but my recollections are only partial and I feel sure there must have been other poets whose work mirrored the lighter side of her personality which have slipped through the memory net.

However, Buntie had several literary friends who used to regale her with their poems – clever and amusing and sometimes about her – and she loved the flow of wit and imagination in the letters that accompanied them. I know she also drew out the same creativity from some of her pupils who might otherwise have been unaware that they possessed such a gift, and encouraged them to meet occasionally in Studio E to share readings and discussion. As far as I know, she herself never attempted to write from her imagination, and if she had would almost certainly have kept it quiet. In fact, it was always her contention that she had no talent for writing. I think she really believed this, and yet the voluminous body of work she has left behind, including notes from her Monday and Saturday groups, to say nothing of her letters and cards to others full of amusing observations, completely contradicts her self-assessment. Her modesty about this was genuine, so she must have judged her own writing by the highest standards.

*

In the course of our long friendship, Buntie and I shared many enthusiasms, but perhaps the one which had the most impact on our lives, and endured the longest, was the love we both felt for Cornwall and the many friends we made there. It began before the war during a hiatus between jobs at Creative Arts, when on a sudden impulse we took the Cornish Riviera Express to Penzance to look for the fishing village of Mousehole and the Wild Birds' Hospital we had read about in Laura Knight's autobiography.

It was a journey which transported us into a world of enchantment, for in a terraced garden high on the hill climbing out of Mousehole and overlooking the blue expanse of Mounts Bay, we came across the Yglesias sisters, the eventual creators of the Wild Birds' Hospital. Their stately mother, formally dressed for the afternoon and wearing an impressive hat swathed in mauve tulle, had come across us, on the doorstep of Cherry Orchard – their home – with a trumped-up enquiry about a cottage to let, and had immediately invited us to tea in the garden. There we found Dorothy in a summer dress and straw hat, and tiny, gnome-like Pog with a huge mop of dark hair in artist's smock and jeans. Surprised but unperturbed by our sudden appearance, they welcomed us with great kindness and thereafter became friends for life. Once our presence was explained, conversation turned naturally to the birds and how a jackdaw with a broken wing, brought to them by a child, had become the first patient in what was to become the Wilds Birds' Hospital, which since had taken over their already busy lives. Soon we were picking our way through the rambling garden among rough bird-houses made by Pog out of packing cases and being introduced to Excelsior the kestrel, Santa Fe the crow, Lazy Daisy the jackdaw and many other aptly-named creatures whose lives had been salvaged by the sisters' loving care. Later on when the birds were again ready to fly, their wings cleaned of oil, we would climb down the cliffs with Dorothy to release them on the rocks below. Some were never seen again; others returned year after year and were welcomed to rest and recuperate before flying off once more.

Their garden, spreading along the hill on several levels was a small paradise, where over the years we spent happy hours working among the proliferation of foliage and flowers and the sounds of innumerable birds, till Dorothy would call us to elevenses or lunch or tea on the lawn. Between Buntie and Pog, who was a woodcarver with an original and eccentric charm, there was a humorous affinity: both were creative and stubbornly individual, and they would exchange sophisticated banter and laughter, and cigarettes tossed from one to the other, Dorothy vainly trying to divert the dubious drift of the conversation. Even now I can visualize them all and recollect the cadence of their three distinctive voices.

For Buntie and me for over thirty years this place became a haven to which we could escape, sometimes together, more often separately, from the pressures of life in London. In the rambling garden were two cottages belonging to the sisters, 'Green Hedges,' and 'Love Lane' where Laura Knight had lived and painted years before and we would stay in whichever was vacant at the time. Although out of sight of each other, they both shared the same unbelievably beautiful, ever-changing prospect of the whole expanse of Mounts Bay, from St. Michael's Mount, round the rocky coast to the Lizard peninsula. It was a magical place to be, whichever cottage one stayed in and a perfect base for exploring the countryside or visiting other close friends in the country beyond Penzance, or just working peacefully in the garden.

Buntie was entranced by the Wild Birds' Hospital and loved both sisters for their selfless dedication to saving the lives of wild creatures. She did all she could to help them, and after Pog died in 1977, went down and took over the daunting task of clearing out her studio, which for years Pog had shared with all her favourite birds. In the following three years until Dorothy died, Buntie spent every Christmas with her and, ignoring all protests, used the holiday to clean the cottage, which Dorothy was too frail to do herself. For Buntie, to be in Cornwall, her favourite place, and to be of use to a loved and greatly respected friend, was for her the most creative way of spending Christmas, whose festivities she had never enjoyed.

*

In the years after the war Buntie and I went our separate ways and both made many new relationships, but our devotion to each other supported us through all the upheavals that occurred in our lives during the following years; perhaps a rather uneven exchange, for my need of support occurred much more often than did hers, and as a loving friend she helped me over many emotional crises as they ebbed and flowed throughout a large part of my life.

Inevitably we met rather less often than before, but there was always the telephone which kept us in touch with each other's activities and whenever possible we exchanged visits.

As time passed I went less often to Cunningham Place and Buntie came more frequently to visit me so that she could get right away from the increasing pressures of her daily life.

We still spent some holidays together, either with our mutual friends in Cornwall or somewhere on the Continent, as well as others with our personal friends. Buntie twice visited Jacky in Athens and often stayed with Yanka Zlatin, either in Paris or at her farmhouse in the Ain region of France. They had a long and fruitful association, for Yanka was a painter and designer and they shared many interests. It is her beautiful painting of 'La Vierge' which now hangs in the new Studio E.

Another friend with whom Buntie had much in common and sometimes went abroad with during the 1960s was Sylvia Wren, a woman of great charm and intelligence who was closely connected with the world of art and music, and lived in a large flat overlooking Hyde Park. She and her flat played a crucial part in Buntie's life when she was very ill with a severe sinus and ear infection, and as usual tried to treat herself rather than consult a doctor. She got steadily worse and Sylvia, taking things into her own hands, without warning turned up at Cunningham Place with a taxi, forced Buntie – protesting – out of bed, into a warm dressing gown, into the taxi and back to her flat. There she sent for a well-known homeopathic doctor who on seeing Buntie's condition immediately contacted an eminent Ear, Nose and Throat specialist who saw her straight away at his home. Because there was no time to lose he dealt with the condition there and then without the facilities of his surgery, a process which later Buntie spoke of as horrifying, and described vividly. Nevertheless he and Sylvia between them had literally saved her life and she was eternally grateful to them both. At the time I happened to be away and on my return, not finding her at Cunningham Place, tracked her down at Sylvia's where she was recuperating. I was shocked at her state and at the whole story, but thankful for Sylvia's initiative and care. Certainly I would not have done as well at that time.

A year or two later, when Sylvia in her turn became very ill and was at first in a London hospital and later in another at St. Albans, Buntie spent all her spare time with her during the agonizing months before her death. Afterwards, worn out and shattered, she took herself to a small Greek island where she could be quite alone, as she did after her mother's death – her usual reaction to grief and loss.

The last two holidays Buntie and I spent together, in 1981-82, were at Salcombe in South Devon where we rented a cottage and had a peaceful time exploring estuaries and islands and the surrounding country and seeing friends who happened to be staying in the neighbourhood as well as her sister Jennie and Roger her husband, who came over from Exeter.

After that we both gravitated towards our families, Buntie spending her holidays with Jennie and Roger and I with Peta my sister, after her husband died.

The last time Buntie and I went anywhere outside London together was in the year before she died, on an excursion to Leeds Castle, said by some to be the loveliest castle in the world. There, after a leafy train journey through the Kent countryside we spent a perfect day, roaming through the park, taking in the rare ducks and geese and swans, a variety of exotic birds, the Culpeper garden and, finally, the ancient castle itself, standing along with all its historic treasures in the surrounding lakes.

We both looked back on this day with such pleasure that we resolved to go there again very soon. Alas, this did not come about because we were never able to fix a day when we were both free at the same time. Perhaps it was just as well; such special happenings can seldom be repeated.

*

42

Buntie always felt most comfortable in casual clothes – loose tops and slacks and sandals – but when seeing patients she took a great deal of trouble over the details of her appearance. In particular it was essential for her to feel at ease about her hair, and a regular appointment with her hairdresser was sacrosanct. For over thirty years she had followed Joyce as she moved from one West End salon to another, and greatly valued their friendly relationship. Even during her illness she insisted on going to see Joyce once more for what she always referred to as her 'hairdo, and remembered her in her will.

During the war and until 1949 when clothes rationing came to an end there was little choice, or money, for buying anything new. Buntie like everyone else found it difficult to find the right clothes until she discovered Galeries Lafayette, a rather exclusive shop in Regent Street which specialised in fashions from Paris. There she found things to wear which suited her. The chic French style was perfect for her curvaceous figure and, until Galeries Lafayette suddenly closed, she went there whenever she needed something new to wear. Its disappearance left a gap in her life and she seldom again found things which she felt were right for her.

As time passed Buntie became more austere with regard to clothes, and food. She acquired a plain dark green coat which appeared to be saying something along the same lines as when she had deliberately abandoned her gold watch as well as her favourite jewellery a few years earlier. The coat she felt happy in and said she enjoyed wearing it. To me it appeared severe and uncompromising and out of character, but I suspect that this determination to rid herself of superfluities was the outcome of her daily readings of the Indian sage, Sri Ramana Maharshi, whose example of austerity and detachment from worldly concerns had become woven into the pattern of her life.

Strangely enough, not long before she became ill she had made for her a beautiful jacket of fine beige leather which delighted her but sadly enough she never had an opportunity to wear it.

It was perhaps for the same reason that she become a strict vegetarian, which did her health no good for such a diet is time-consuming to prepare and she told me she was often too tired to bother. Even the food placed in the little cupboard on the landing outside her door by her concerned friends did not always get eaten: one good reason I felt it was important for her to have meals with me at weekends whenever she was free and I was at home.

In later years Buntie allowed herself less and less time for the interests which had always been part of her life: painting, theatre, music, exhibitions. Occasionally she would slip away to see a film which had caught her interest and talk about it later with enthusiasm, or cross Piccadilly after a 'hairdo' to see an exhibition at the Royal Academy; she always knew what was worth seeing. She had a deep love and appreciation of painting and could see behind the subject and discover qualities that the painter had been unaware of. As Catherine Yarrow, a pupil and artist, wrote, 'Buntie had "perfect pitch" for modern art and this was like a miracle for me.' Her working life seemed to stretch; there was so often someone in desperate straits who had to be fitted in to an already crowded programme. Even Sundays were not sacrosanct and when not working on a talk for a group, she would often see someone in need. But whenever she was free of such pressures she would come over to a meal with me and play Scrabble, which was for her a refreshment because it drove out all other preoccupations. Even when she was very ill she wanted to play and she nearly always won.

*

In the past Buntie had told me that just as she worked out appropriate homeopathic remedies for her patients, she did the same for herself whenever she had symptoms of illness. Often she stayed up all night to take them at the prescribed intervals to make sure she would be fit to see patients the following day. But the time came in the summer of 1985 when the remedies she had been taking for a persistent cough did not have any effect; the cough did not go away.

Since early in May I had noticed when we met that she often seemed tired and sometimes distracted, although she did not admit to being unwell. This could have been because for several months I was going frequently to Croydon where my brother was very ill and needing help with moving from his house, and she would not have wished to cause me further anxiety. Typically, she even offered to help by going instead of me.

It was not until the beginning of July that she admitted that her troublesome cough was getting worse rather than better, and decided to seek the advice of a homeopathic doctor she had often consulted about her pupils This led to x-rays, a provisional diagnosis by her G.P., and through him a referral to the Royal Marsden Hospital for further investigation. On the day she was to hear the result, I went with her to the hospital. She was with the consultant for an hour, and did not speak at all going back in the taxi or for some time afterwards: I could only imagine what she was going through. Eventually she was able to tell me that the diagnosis was cancer of the lungs, and that she had at the most only a few months to live. Then, once the worst had been assimilated, it was for her a matter of being practical.

She came to stay in my secluded flat where she could be certain of privacy, always essential for her. She was thankful to be away from Landseer Studios which was vulnerable to intruders: the front door was often left unlatched and people could walk in and up the stairs, and frequently did.

For a time she hoped for some unorthodox cure or at least for a remission, and would not allow anyone, even her family, to know the truth about her illness. Enquiries had to be dissembled until she was ready to accept that there was no hope of cure. Once she had accepted this, she went from time to time to Cunningham Place and set about putting her affairs in order with the help of her friends there. Nearly every day Mary Ann Ephgrave, who was acting as secretary to the groups, brought piles of letters for her to deal with. Apart from her, visitors to do with her physical state, and later her family, she would see almost no one, true to her deep need for privacy at times of crisis.

Frail though she was by then, in September Buntie insisted on going for the holiday in Devon which had been planned the previous year when she, Jennie and Roger had seen a delightful hotel on the banks of the River Tavy and had booked to stay there the following autumn. She had looked forward to this holiday ever since. On the day they set out, Buntie declined my offer of help with packing and very slowly, with her usual precision, dealt with it herself. On her return two weeks later she was visibly weaker but insisted on climbing the stairs up to my flat on the third floor without help.

Gradually Buntie's strength diminished. She was never bedridden but always up and dressed, spending most of the day in an armchair where she loved to watch the changing sky, the birds and the trees in the Square and the abundant flowers at the windows. To me it seemed that over the years flowers had become an extension of her personality, and she always lavishly decorated her own domain as well as dispatching flowers with a personal message to anyone she cared about who was ill or distressed, or celebrating anniversaries.

After Buntie returned from Devon, Hope Shaw, a friend of many years who was a physiotherapist, arranged for us to have practical help from the then newly-opened Hospice of

St. John and St. Elizabeth. The MacMillan nurse, Margaret O'Grady, called frequently and was a cheering influence, kind and resourceful; it is hard to imagine what we would have done without her. And it was comforting to know that there would be a bed for Buntie at the hospice if that became necessary, as eventually it did. Often she suffered discomfort and pain, and breathing became difficult for her, although she seldom complained but remained silent and stoical. At times when she was unable to sleep she would come into the sitting room where I slept and sit by the fire. We might have tea and talk or just sit quietly until she felt able to go back to bed and perhaps sleep.

On the few occasions when I had to go away, to my sister in Sussex or to my brother's funeral in Hampshire, Jennie came from Exeter to take care of her. For me it was a great relief to know that Buntie was in loving hands, and for them it was an opportunity to be alone together and talk without distraction at this critical period of their lives.

During her illness, the meditation group arranged regular sessions at the beginning and end of each day, sessions in which Buntie and I joined until the time came when she was too weak to take part. Then she asked to hear readings from Julian of Norwich or *Talking with Angels* or from *The Bible*, which helped to sustain us both.

Perhaps Toni Sussman's most precious legacy to Buntie was the teaching of Sri Ramana Maharshi, who became her Guru as he had been Toni's. It appears that in a dream she saw Ramana behind Toni's chair, and the next day went out and bought all the books by and about him that she could find. After that, it was for years her practice to get up early each morning to read Ramana's works in preparation for the coming day, and while she was with me she asked for a large picture of him to be placed where she could always see it. And it was his shining face, placed at the end of her bed, which was with her at the hospice during the last three days of her life.

Among Ramana's works I came across these words which I feel express the significance of Buntie's life:

Whatever one gives to others is in truth given to oneself; once this is understood how can one refuse anything to another?

*

Gabrielle Boole

The young Buntie aged about 10, with her younger sister Jennie.

"I was once a raving beauty, and extremely wicked!"

The working commercial artist in pre-war Studio E, on the
mantelpiece a photograph of her mother.
Below – with friend and colleague Gabrielle Boole.

Buntie the Land Girl in the Forestry Service, 1940
near right with head scarf and hands stretched toward the fire.

Buntie by Buntie, on holiday in France in the 1950s.

10^A Cunningham Place photographed in 1975.

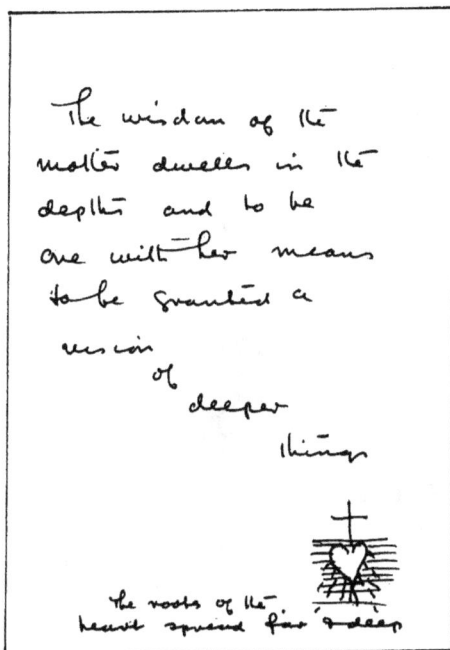

The wisdom of the mother dwells in the depths and to be one with her means to be granted a vision of deeper things

the roots of the heart spread far & deep

A typical communication from Buntie, with a cross she often drew.

WHEN THE WIND OF RIGHT KNOWLEDGE
HAS BLOWN AWAY THE CLOUDS OF ILLUSION
NOTHING ELSE
IS REQUIRED
TO MAKE THE SUN
SHINE.
IT HAS BEEN THERE ALL THE TIME!
THE SELF HAS ALWAYS BEEN REALISED
WE HAVE ALWAYS BEEN FREEDOM ITSELF
BHAGAVAN SAID "GET RID OF THE IDEA THAT YOU HAVE NOT REALIZED."

A card of the teachings of Sri Ramana Maharshi, one of many
written for the meditation group.

Portrait of Buntie by Eileen Chandler, 1961.

II HER WORK WITH INDIVIDUALS

BEGINNINGS

A spreading network brought people of all ages and types, from Britain and abroad, to sit with Buntie Wills in her small room in St. Johns Wood. Some simply knocked on her door because they had heard about her; some met her in the street, on a train, or sitting under a tree. Others came because they knew someone who was already seeing her. Seldom did they come through formal referral or 'recommendation.'

*

Buntie once told me that she believed everyone who arrived on her doorstep was meant to be there. In all her years, she said, only once had she to send someone away – and in that instance, she was needed to push them gently towards their true destination.

*

I was at the Manjushri Institute in Cumbria, a Tibetan Buddhist centre, and there she was. I used to see her in the corridor during the meditation course, always with her arm around somebody. In that self-contained place, I thought, 'That's very nice.'

I saw her again at various times. I was having a particularly bad time in a relationship, when I met her on a day course run by the Sufi, Pir Vilat Khan. I saw her there and suddenly clicked: 'Buntie, I think I have to come and see you,' and she said, 'I've been waiting for years!' She knew long before I did: she was just biding her time for me to ask.

She later told me, 'I have to spend half my life just waiting.'

*

The headmistress of my daughter's school realised the family was in a bad way and suggested coming to see this Buntie Wills. I was a bit reluctant, and I didn't get in touch for another year. She said, 'It was right for you to come now, when you did.'

*

I am not going to pretend that any of the things I have come to know about Buntie, and about myself for that matter, were even a glimmer in my consciousness when I ended up going to see her. A relationship had failed, something that had never occurred to me could happen, and I didn't know what to do. I just had an instinct that unless I got some help, I'd keep on repeating this pattern. I was living in a house with someone who was seeing Buntie, who was also the first person I'd ever met who ate brown rice and yoghurt. This woman said, 'I know someone who might help you. I think you'd suit.' I discovered she had Jungian tendencies, though I had no idea what that meant. My best friend in the States had ended up in therapy, while I'd never heard the word before, and she had cautioned me, 'Look for a Jungian, stay away from Freudians.'

I wrote to this woman Buntie Wills and then made an appointment. I think my first feeling, the first time the door was opened at Cunningham Place, was quite frankly one of disappointment. I was into women's liberation and

56

community work and here was this proper, posh-ish looking older woman, with neat white hair and none of the gush I was used to as an American.

It is easy with hindsight to see what kept me going to see her, but at the time I didn't have a clue. As Buntie once commented to me about how I got to this country and then to her, 'Ah, not by accident my sweetheart. By appointment.'

I had the idea that after a while I would be 'better' and go back to life as it had been. I did not even admit to my closest friends that I was seeing someone for therapy. People at work, when they saw me, a workaholic, disappear at the same time each Tuesday, speculated on whether I was having an affair or kindly visiting some elderly invalid.

*

In 1957 I had a nervous breakdown, and went to Buntie whom I knew slightly. I was in urgent need of help, which no one else could give me. Although the day that I phoned her was, for her, a normally busy one, she managed to find time to give me an appointment on the same day. She saw me daily for the next eight days including Thursday, which I did not then know was her free day, and Sunday. Much later she told me that I had been one of four people who called her on that day, all with breakdowns, wanting to see her as soon as possible.

*

It was in a state of deep distress that a watching, knowing friend found me late one September night. 'I know what's happening to you,' she said, and I replied, 'I'm glad you do because I don't understand any of this.' She said that she knew someone who could help me. I agreed to go to her if it could be arranged. Next morning the friend called for me early, carrying a basket. She said an appointment had been arranged for 4.30 that afternoon, not far away – and that in the meantime we were going to Kew Gardens for a picnic. We did, and then she duly accompanied me to the front door of 10 Cunningham Place at the appointed time.

My friend was not an imaginative person. It is only recently that I have realized the picnic shows Buntie's invisible hand. She had suggested that my friend keep me occupied all day, so that I couldn't change my mind and miss the opportunity of starting my new psychological life.

*

I was at a very low ebb and I had gone as far as I could in a situation when I suddenly broke down at a friend's and that friend directed me to Buntie. I went to see her and when I entered the place, I was put in the waiting room by the secretary. Then Buntie came in and asked, What is your name?' and I said, 'Green,' in a very aggressive and churlish manner. She replied in a gentle voice, 'And what is your first name?'

Although for some time after I still behaved in a strange way, gradually Buntie won me over completely and I became very attached to her.

*

It would not be right to leave the impression that Buntie was everyone's cup of tea. I recommended a couple of friends for whom she just did not click. They found her a slightly repetitive old lady and wondered why I raved about her.

*

Buntie once told me that someone came to see her thinking she was a fortune teller, because she had misunderstood what a friend had told her about Buntie. It took several sessions before this lady realized her mistake.

*

I had just moved into a new flat, my first, and my best friend was over from the States. I invited Buntie over, not realizing that she seldom went out. She came and met my friend, who immediately knew she wanted to work with Buntie. She later flew over several times a year, and this connection led to other 'American sweethearts' doing the same.

I felt that Buntie had come to visit because she knew it was important, somehow. The next time I saw Buntie she said, 'I won't see your friend unless it's OK with you. I don't want anything to harm our work together.' She already sensed rivalry between us. I would not have said 'no' but I felt valued and cherished at her recognition.

*

I was wanting Buntie to see a friend of mine but she said, 'No, I'm not going to do it because it wouldn't be good for *you* if I did.'

*

On a certain morning the phone rings in Cunningham Place. A female voice asks, 'Can I speak to Miss Wills?' Buntie answers, 'Miss Wills speaking.'

The voice continues: 'This is Doctor X's secretary. Hold the line, the doctor would like to speak to you.'

Eventually the doctor speaks: "Miss Wills? I hear that you see psychologically disturbed people . . . ' .

She answered, 'There is some mistake. I do not see psychologically disturbed people. I only see people.'

*

There are a number of words which Buntie very deliberately did not use. 'Disease' is one of them. The nearest she ever got to using it was as a hyphenated word: Dis-ease, making certain to emphasis the hyphenated nature of the word.

*

From first knowing that I was going to meet Buntie to actually meeting her took me all of a year. I hesitated for twelve months because I had heard so much about her and her pupils that I felt that in order to become her pupil you had to be in some way 'wonderful.' The more I heard about her, the more I secretly wanted to meet her, but I was convinced that I was utterly worthless and certainly not nearly 'wonderful' enough. The accounts that I had been given were actually fair, because everyone who went to see Buntie became 'wonderful.' That is to say that she brought out the wonder and the wondrous in all of us, for that was her remarkable gift.

When I finally met her and told her I felt myself to be devoid of worth or talent, she gave me her gentle, authoritative reassurance that everybody has talent for something, that everybody has a place in the order of things. No one had ever said that to me before and yet, to my surprise, I believed her immediately. I knew she was right.

In addition, there was the matter of Buntie's being a psychiatrist of some sort. I had never actually met a psychiatrist but I had nevertheless developed a profound distaste for them and their trade. During my year's hesitation, it had become clear from the accounts of friends that Buntie Wills was something other – and more – than a psychiatrist.

60

Wills was something other – and more – than a psychiatrist. One friend asked me how I pictured her and I said that I had little idea of what she might look like, except that I knew her eyes would be extraordinary. And I was right, her eyes *were* extraordinary.

*

How had I come to see Buntie in the first place? Why go to London for therapy when you live in Western Massachusetts? I had had five years of Freudian therapy, at various stages of my life. During treatment I found that my state of mind would improve, but when I stopped I would sink back into my familiar patterns of depression and inefficiency, haunted by feelings of futility and helplessness. Despondency was my usual state.

I had just about decided that there was no remedy, that I would have to live with this gloomy, tiresome self, when I noticed that among my friends who were seeing therapists, there was one who was changing more interestingly and more substantially than anyone else. What was her secret? I asked.

My friend told me that every sabbatical leave, winter break, and summer vacation she spent in London seeing a woman who practised Jungian therapy but in an idiosyncratic, highly intuitive style that was all her own. She was a remarkable healer, my friend said. 'Might I have her address?' I asked. I might. So my next sabbatical found me in London, waiting to see Buntie.

*

61

To seek to know the significance of life
is itself the result of good karma in past births.
Those who do not seek such knowledge
are simply wasting their lives.

Sri Ramana Maharshi

GETTING THERE

For many who knew Buntie, getting to her house was an integral part of the therapy session. Now a listed building, No. 10a Cunningham Place, just off the Edgware Road, was a square Victorian double-fronted house which had seen better days. Stone steps led up to a pillared portico and a front door with opaque inset glass and a row of doorbells. The ground floor was a network of studios and the smell of linseed oil greeted you as you entered. Landseer the engraver, brother of the famous painter, had once lived and worked there, and Queen Victoria had visited him as a pupil. As well as a distinguished sculptor, there was a convivial family of picture restorers who carried on their business in the house plus a painter and glass engraver.

Buntie's domain was on the upper floor, reached by a returning flight of stairs. She lived and worked in only three rooms – her consulting room, the waiting room, and her living room which was also her bedroom and office. In the mid-70s she acquired Studio E on the ground floor, where she had earlier worked as an artist and which she then used for groups. All of these rooms she rented from a series of landlords.

*

I was very nervous the first time I went to see her, and very excited. Who was this strange lady I'd heard so much about? Already she'd asked for, and I'd written, big swatches of autobiographical manuscript. 'Tell me about yourself,' she'd said, 'from 0-7 years, from 7-14 years, from 14-21 years.' (Apparently the seventeen years since then didn't interest her so much.) At her request eighty pages of handwritten prose had come spilling out and been sent off to her. I'd also sent, as instructed, a list of the books that had influenced me most in my life. And I had read her suggested preparation for our meeting, *The Inner World of Choice* by Frances Wickes, and *Knowing Woman: A Feminine Psychology* by Irene Claremont de Castillejo. Both books were discussions from a Jungian point of view of the difficulties and complexities that come into being as a human life unfolds. As Jungians tend to be, they were more interested in the inescapable challenges of maturation that everyone confronts than in what we would call neurosis or mental disease. I had read these books with my heart; they were moving as well as illuminating. Now I was to meet the woman who'd sent me to them, and whose instruction was already beginning its powerful imp act on my life.

The day was radiantly sunny. 'A good omen,' she said. September 30th. It turned out to be her birthday. I took the tube from Notting Hill Gate to Paddington, and then to Warwick Avenue. There was a section of old canal on the way to Buntie's studio, houseboats lining one side, ducks swimming along the other, borders of large trees overhanging. It was a place that seemed to me to slip out of time, a thread of the past embedded in the present, always peaceful, always lovely. The walk became part of the experience of seeing her. Somehow it distilled the essence of whatever it meant to see her, inviting the act of attentiveness she encouraged in her teaching.

I rang the bell and waited, wondering. Through the glass of the door I could see a dim shape coming down the stairs. The door was opened by a tiny woman with brilliant blue eyes and hair of silver white – Buntie herself. 'So,' she said, taking both my hands and leaning back to have a better look, 'This is Joan.' 'Yes,' I replied. 'Greetings,' she said, and put her arms around me. (What a contrast, I thought, to the tall grey Freudian analyst who in five years barely even shook my hand and who I knew primarily as the toe of a shoe glimpsed out of the corner of my eye when I lay on the Freudian couch.) Taking me by the hand again, she led me up the curved flight of stairs (she was never afraid to treat her pupils as children – I don't mean in a condescending way, but with a matter-of-fact maternity that reached the child hidden inside) and ushered me into her waiting room.

*

The session for me started outside the front door. My heart began to beat heavily in anticipation and was only stilled by the hazy vision of her descending the stairs to let me in.

*

What I remember so clearly is the feeling of security and happiness when, after pushing the door bell at   10a Cunningham Place, I could see and hear Buntie coming down the stairs at the end of the hallway, to open the glazed front door. I remember two things: the smell of linseed oil or floor polish, and the smile on Buntie's face, her very particular smile which included a touch of wickedness, of irony, of scepticism and tolerance, but which in any case made you feel welcome and secure.

*

65

The warmth of that welcome was so strong. Her leading me up the stairs was so like images I had in dreams before and after I met her, of a wise old woman leading me somewhere safe and exciting.

*

Buntie seemed quite grand in her bearing. She would open the door, take me by the hand, and lead me up the stairs; she was first grand and then very cosy.

*

I saw Buntie in 'term time' approximately once every three weeks, on a Saturday. In a very short time the 'lady in London' became someone of great importance in my life, to be remembered with deep affection and esteem. I have a strong composite memory of my visits to Cunningham Place and the kind of rituals they entailed. For many of them I arrived at ten o'clock on a Saturday morning, one of the no-secretary days. I would ring the bell and listen for the footsteps coming down the stairs. Sometimes, Buntie's voice would tell me that the front door was still locked from the inside and she would have to go and fetch the key. Then, after the key had turned, her bright eyes would take in whether I was having a good or bad day and her two hands would clasp my right hand and draw me in through the doorway. Sometimes I would be clutching her pint of milk from the doorstep in my other hand. Or, on occasions when I brought flowers, perhaps lily of the valley or rose-buds from the garden, she would accept them as if they were the best flowers ever. Acceptance was one of the keynotes with Buntie. I felt that if I had stepped into the hall and told her I had just murdered someone she would have looked at me calmly and invited me upstairs to talk about it. I guess I felt a bit like a primary school pupil taking flowers for the teacher, which is what Buntie so eminently was.

*

On many occasions I came to the door of Cunningham Place in a state of anxiety and distress, my mind full of problems. Having rung the bell, I would hear the firm, serene footfalls. I would hear the latch click, and then a welcoming hand would greet me and draw me into the hall, Buntie would pick up a pile of mail and then with the same firm, serene step lead the way upstairs. By the time I found myself sitting opposite her the serenity and love in her footfall alone had already alleviated my anguish and distress, so I could speak.

*

Shortly before I became brave enough actually to ring the bell, I was passing Landseer Studios late one night. I climbed the front steps just to have a look and found a bell push marked b wills. That floored me. This was the late sixties and it was trendy to discard the use of capital letters in proper names. I was suddenly unsure about this b wills. Was she a trendy, or did she just have insufficient Letraset? After a further week's hesitation it was time to press the bell. In daylight this time and with heart pounding I pushed the button, and somewhere inside the building a bell rang. I felt sick. I wanted to unpush the button and unring the bell and go back to my procrastination. This was not possible, the bell had rung and there was no going back. That very moment someone inside the building was getting out of a chair. I had started. The apprenticeship had begun and I was learning my first lesson about cause and effect.

Noel, Buntie's secretary, came to the door. Miss Wills was booked up for weeks, if not months. There were, of course, occasional cancellations, but things did not look hopeful. My name would go on a list, but I must be prepared to wait. I had known it all along – I was worthless, I was not going to meet her and that was how it ought to be, she was far too busy to see me and I had been very foolish ever to think otherwise. I ought to go home and forget it all. I had a lousy day and it was evening when I got back to the London suburb that served as my home at the time. In the hallway was a telegram with my name on it. I opened it. It was from Buntie, and I had an appointment the following morning at eleven o'clock.

The next morning I was there punctually and pressed the bell again – this time with the slightly increased self-assurance afforded by an official appointment. Buntie descended the stairs in the way that has made many of our hearts quicken over the years, greeted me with the words,'Well . . . at last!' and taking my hand, led me upstairs to her consulting room, sat me in the chair opposite her and asked me why I had come to see her. I could hardly speak at this point; I had seen something in Buntie that I had needed all my life and that I had been waiting for until that moment. It was of course in the eyes that I saw the extra dimension which made sense of all other things and breathed life into them. The need to reach out to that dimension was surely the most profound impulse in all living creatures, for the sake of which even rats will abandon food and procreation. I urgently needed to explore that new corridor and here at last was someone who could take me there.

*

I used to look at and marvel at Buntie's note to the postman attached right under the bell I had just pressed. It told him in no uncertain terms that she did not want the mail addressed to the basement pushed through her letter box. No cringing

68

or social politeness here. Had she done an assertiveness training course? This note was a perpetual reminder to me that behind the warmth, wit and caring was an extremely strong, independently-minded woman indeed.

*

Buntie was and is very much the tree in whose arms I went to be, like the tree she had told me once grew on the site where Studio E now was, the tree which she felt grew up through her chair and in whose arms we all rested. Problems that had loomed large became part of the whole. Climbing the stairs to her waiting room, having been let in by her, began the journey. From the moment of seeing her I was aware of her profound power of presence. A power that was never used as a weapon, but served the heart and thereby the truth.

*

Your quest is your work now.
Allow yourself to be a pilgrim.

WAITING

The waiting room was very still and for many, a place of significance. It was small and cheerful with an orange glow about it. Bookcases stretched from floor to ceiling along the far wall, there was a large Russian ikon, a photograph of C.G. Jung, prints and original paintings, and a number of interesting small symbolic items. It was furnished simply, with one or two comfortable chairs and a coffee table covered in books and brochures.

*

The tranquillity that emanated from Buntie (I never saw her hurry or look ruffled in spite of the enormous numbers of people she must have seen) was reflected in the rooms she provided. Everything – the books and pictures, the carpets and chairs, the pottery and sculptures, the postcards, the scents (I always gently coveted a round Italian box filled with perfumed wood shavings) and above all the beloved flowers, both in the waiting room and in the consulting room: all these created an atmosphere of beauty which was luminous and peaceful.

*

I recall Buntie telling me that in the sixties it was one of her few personal pleasures to get up early in the morning and take time to arrange flowers for her rooms. She said that after all her years as an artist and designer, it was the only artistic activity she had in her present life.

*

The waiting room was in whites and red, walls white, red in the chairs and carpeting – warm, bright, sunny. A stained glass angel hung in the window. There were all sorts of books to look at and read: a collection of Rembrandt's drawings, a book on meditation, a book on child care centres, another on therapeutic uses of music, a collection of cartoons about the perplexities of being a liberated woman. The room was an invitation to peaceful unhurried reflection, to pausing. It was a reception room that felt receptive.

*

She always left a new person in the waiting room a very long time because she wanted to see them as they were and not as they wanted to present themselves.

It was important to wait. You learn from waiting, she said.

*

I often had to wait a very long time in the waiting room – sometimes an hour – and I used to remind myself that this was because there was someone with Buntie who was in great need. I knew, too, that she would have given me the same extra time if I really needed it.

*

Always concerned with the value of my own time, I found the waiting room an irritation. And then I realized the waiting room could be put to use. When Buntie started the meditation group she taught us that every moment we were waiting was an opportunity for meditation. I began to use the waiting room for just that purpose. One day, I sat there in meditation and in due course the door opened and Buntie came in to fetch me. Her hand still on the doorknob, she said, 'Ah, I hadn't intended to disrupt the guru.' Immediately I felt foolish, I thought it was a leg-pull. So I countered, 'Buntie, I do the funnies around here.' And she said, 'No dearest, the guru is always present and when you meditate, he is particularly strongly present.'

*

There were always books and magazines in Buntie's waiting room, but I always wondered how anyone could possibly read while they sat there. I was too busy trying to be calm, and marshalling all the things bursting out of me to be said. The only thing in the room that ever really drew my attention was the picture over the mantelpiece – an ikon of the Nativity. We talked of it one day and Buntie explained that it represented the birth after the waiting. She added that our waiting was just as important as the sessions with her, and that much inner work was done in that room before joining her.

*

When I first went to see Buntie I was running this unit for teenagers at King's Cross and so needless to say I was extremely important and extremely busy. Buntie was never ever on time and as I had the last appointment on a Tuesday evening I would let my timing slide. My appointment was initially 6.30 so I drove up at 6.30 or 6.40 or sometimes it was 6.45. Usually it was not until at least 7 p.m. that I would see her. She finally told me off one day, with great sternness. 'The waiting is as important as seeing me,' she said. 'Besides, when you ring that bell, it is a signal to me to begin to finish with the person before you.' That really brought me up short. I had thought, 'I'm not wasting my time sitting in that waiting room.'

*

I loved her waiting room. It was an Aladdin's cave of fascinating things to look at: sweethearts' drawings (often with Buntie's text attached), paintings, plasticine sculptures, and on the main table, a mass of leaflets and books, all of which were relevant or took you on a journey through some new, exciting territory. Many of these books and pamphlets had been given to Buntie by her sweethearts – tokens of their creativity and inner worlds, projects they were running, courses they were holding. Buntie was into 'networking' – putting people in touch with each other – long before anyone had heard of the term.

*

Never fear chaos – for out of chaos something is always born. Instead of worrying – await the birth . . . !

73

STARTING SESSIONS

The muted sounds of conversation on the outside landing signalled that the previous person was leaving and the next session was about to begin. Buntie herself led her pupil into the small consulting room. It was painted a dusky rose and contained a large wooden chest of drawers, a divan covered with books and pupils' work. Beside the gas fire on shelves were the complete works of C.G. Jung and on the mantelpiece, an exquisite arrangement of flowers, leaves and branches. There were also unusual stones and 'objets trouvés' of great meaning, both to Buntie and to those who gave them to her.

She sat in a large upholstered chair by the window, its arms worn thin from years of use. The pupil sat in a deep balloon-backed Victorian armchair opposite her. Near her feet was a footstool, to use if you needed to come closer.

*

Walking from the waiting room to the consulting room, Buntie said to me, 'You see, dearest, this is the only logical course of action for an intelligent man to take.'

*

74

The first time I met Buntie, I was half an hour late. But she still gave me an hour and a half, without the slightest hint of the condemnation my fear was expecting. We did not talk intensively; she was too much at ease for that. She was interested not only in me, but in my wife and children, asking for their names, descriptions, photographs. She was the parodox of a genuinely comforting lady who was as deeply concerned for my truth as The Truth. Perhaps (I only knew her in her old age) she was a little didactic and repetitive at times, but with her there was never any chance of disguising the truth under emotional flannel or verbal jargon. Buntie would say, 'People don't want your time – they want your Self'

*

At the first session I had with Buntie after months of waiting to get there I was quaking inside. She asked me why I had come. I didn't really know in words but took out a painting that had 'painted itself' six months before.

It was of a strange almost bird-shaped woman on one leg: her arms seemed part of the main body like wings, her head almost tucked away. Inside the body was a tiny egg inside of which was a small person. The ground all around was cracked like an earthquake, black cracks on white paper.

She nodded. I knew she understood from that moment. She explained how the 'pavement' between our conscious and unconscious cracks and the inner and outer world make contact, the contact also between the head and the heart. It was such a relief. I had thought I was going insane.

Buntie then drew a picture for me, of the cross with a heart at its centre. The cross had roots going through the cracked pavement into the ground. The tree. So it was all right for my pavement to crack. This was a real beginning of finding me, that little person inside, and of growing my tree.

I did not go to see Buntie: she came to see me.

I was in a sanatorium and one of the nurses sent a message to Buntie to say there was a patient in great psychological distress, could she come and see if she could do something. I had said I would see someone, then my Scottishness came out and I refused to see her. I wrote a letter cancelling her visit but she appeared in my room shortly after and sat down at the end of the bed. From a terrible feeling of stress and utter despair, I then experienced the utter relief, as of drowning and all of a sudden finding someone to hold on to.

She had only been there a minute and a half when the door opened and my brother came in. I had been in hospital a year and a half and he had never before visited. Buntie did not say a word: she just rose with her umbrella and walked out of the door.

The next day she was there again. She sat at the foot of my bed. In the sanatorium there were framed Medici prints; someone came round every week and you could choose the print you wanted. That week I'd chosen Rouault's *Old King*. Buntie just sat there and said,'You'll see, dearest, the time will come when the whole pattern will fall into place, just like that picture.'

*

I started to write, 'One met Buntie,' or 'One used to say to Buntie,' but then remembered the first time I went to Buntie, explaining to her why I needed to see her, when she said quite sharply, 'Stop saying "one does this and one does that," and say *I*.'

At that time, in my late thirties, my eyes were closed to almost everything that Buntie represented so that whatever she said to me and showed me came as a revelation. Now it is difficult to recapture the freshness and wonder of what she revealed in those short 60 minute sessions in the little first floor room in Cunningham Place. Sometimes I left walking on air, sometimes I left so racked by emotion that it was difficult to go on to some other meeting or task without some space in between to recover.

Buntie demanded my whole attention. She knew immediately if mentally and spiritually I was with her that day or if my mind was wandering. She had her own circular way of meeting me perhaps by talking herself for three-quarters of the time about matters or memories that seemed to me to be quite irrelevant to the urgent issues that I wanted to tell her about, and then right at the end letting me talk, or referring to a dream I had sent her. I assumed that all therapists worked like that but now I realize that Buntie had her own very special way of interrelating with each person who went to see her.

*

Eyes, deep and mysterious, looking into me. 'How are you?' And suddenly my protective walls collapse and I am in tears, spilling all over the room – water – distress welling up from a bottomless pit. The self-sufficient form that walked into the house has disintegrated. I did think that I existed before, but now where am I?

She stores my dreams in her filing system. She is wise – she sees how I could be. She is practised. She shows me how . . . my feeble efforts to breathe . . . to fill out my narrow and wobbly self, give her more joy than I am capable of realizing. I am still living in a half-light, struggling through a mist. Unaware of anything much at all – most of all blind. She can see.

*

I was hysterical and desperate. I'd been to one doctor after another, including a famous hospital, and all anyone had done for me was to send me to someone else. My appointment with Buntie was not until the afternoon, and it was hard to get through the day till then.

What I said during that first session is mercifully lost, as Buntie did not tape-record. What remains with me is the feeling that at last I've got somebody who takes me seriously (even if I'm talking a lot of nonsense), who does not send me away to someone else, and whom I shall go on seeing as long as I need to. I know myself to be in a state where I can't be responsible; at last I've found someone who will take on responsibility for me as long as it is necessary.

*

The most unique feature I felt in Buntie was her complete acceptance of me as someone to be loved and cared for, and her absolute lack of any judging. It was completely safe for me to tell Buntie anything and everything.

*

How did a session with Buntie proceed? With my previous analyst, I would wait to see what came to mind and drone on about it, in a lengthy, self-pitying monologue. When I saw other therapists, I usually went with something in mind, some problem I wanted to talk about. With Buntie I sometimes did the same thing, but more often it was she who determined the flow of conversation. Sometimes she talked more than I did. She thought of herself as both healer and teacher – and was. In the first few minutes of a session she would try to 'feel' where I was. The sense she got would then direct what she said. Once when I was drenched in melancholy, she said, 'Describe one of your favourite walks.' I told her about one of the walks I sometimes take through scrubby woodlands and grasslands and over the dunes by the sea. 'Good,' she said. 'That's something you can do when you're depressed. Take a walk in your mind. You'll find that it helps.'

*

When she asked me why I had come to see her, she stared at me with those piercing eyes. I was very defensive yet I didn't mind a bit, I trusted her completely. Her head moved slowly from side to side, her eyes continued to look into me, and I felt I hardly needed to answer her question because she was drawing out so much information about my distress and my misery and as she did so, she replaced it with compassion. Unable to express my sense of worthlessness, of futility, of emptiness, I began to weep. I told her I felt empty, with nothing inside, just a wasteland. As if when I looked at my arm, it was just anybody's arm and there was nothing inside. She replied very quietly that tears did not mean there was nothing inside. That was the best news I'd ever heard. She went on to say that she could not help me directly but she could help me to help myself and that she could do so as long as I felt I needed it and that when she had given me all she possessed and I wanted to look further, it would be time to look further. Even then, such extraordinary modesty.

In that first session she told me that she intended to cut my head off. I knew intuitively what she meant. After that I didn't remember much of the day, but colours were brighter, there was a poignancy. My life began that day.

*

When Buntie had started working as a therapist, but was still under Toni Sussman's supervision, she complained one day to Toni that she really was having a problem having to listen to so much 'chitty-chat' from people when they first came to her, going over the petty surface details of their life when she

79

was so ready to meet them in depth. Telling the story against herself, Buntie related that Toni gave her a firm ticking off, and told her that what she called 'chitty-chat' was very important, and that she should listen to it carefully no matter how many visits it took. 'It is through you really listening to the chitty-chat that they will learn they can trust you,' said Toni.

*

Buntie used to irritate me sometimes by launching into small talk at the beginning of a session. She'd chat about this and that – and often the subject was herself. I used to think, resentfully, that this was my session and I had many urgent issues to talk about and why was she wasting time in idle conversation. Later, she told me that small talk was necessary to get the true rapport going, to give space to get to know each other properly and afresh each time. Since I always left every session feeling calmer and clearer, one has to concede that whatever the appearance, Buntie was definitely in control of proceedings from beginning to end.

*

At my first visit to Buntie, she began it with the words, 'Tell me a bit about yourself, dear.' I talked for an hour (and sobbed through most of it) while she asked an occasional question. Then at the end she said gently, 'Y-es . . . I can see several patterns there I think we can work on together. Can you come and see me on . . . ?'

*

The first time I went to see Buntie she told me quite clearly, 'I can't change you. I cannot help you solve your problems. But I can help you re-solve them.'

80

*

At my very first session, my life in chaos and feeling in shreds, I wailed, 'Oh Buntie, I can't do anything right: everything I do seems to create more chaos.'
'Stop *doing*, dearest,' she said, 'and start *being*.'

*

The most powerful work I did with Buntie was of course the face-to-face encounters in her little room; sometimes with very little said but so much felt in the powerful silence of 'just being' together.

*

*And all shall be well, and all shall be well,
and all manner of thing shall be well.*

St. Julian of Norwich

STORIES

Buntie was an inveterate story teller. She would tell stories to illustrate a point, help you realize something more clearly, or crystallize a conversation – and sometimes she told them simply to relax people and make them laugh. They could be classical fairy tales, anecdotes she had gleaned over many years, or stories about herself and her own experience. Sometimes they were allegorical or enigmatic, leaving the individual to work out or ponder over what relevance such a story might have to her or his own problems. She imbued them with dramatic meaning and delivered them with perfect timing.

She made the stories fit the circumstances of each pupil. This is only a sample selection of her vast repertoire.

*

The Tibetans Buddhists teach by repetition and Buntie had such an affinity for them. I felt the same way about her stories as I did theirs. Often even the same sentence would be repeated time after time. It is part of an ancient teaching tradition that you also find in children's stories.

She often used fairy tales. She used to tell me over and over again the story of Beauty and the Beast, and to a friend of mine, the Snow Queen. It was pure psychology about male sexuality: she was trying to get me to incorporate a part of the

maleness that I was not so comfortable with. I'm still trying to work on it. The fact is that I have never forgotten it. Her repetition meant it
went in deep.

*

I remember apologizing for crying and Buntie saying, 'Those are tears from the heart, my sweetheart, not tears of self-pity. Like the boy in the fairy tale about the Snow Queen, who was able to cry when the ice – his heart – melted.' And she sent me off to read the Snow Queen.

*

There was a story about the writer Colette, who went for an evening walk in Paris with her husband. When eventually Colette turned and began to retrace their steps, her husband didn't want to go back along the same street, saying that they had already seen it.

'How can you say that?' cried Colette, 'Look at it – the light is on the other side now; and that cat wasn't on the wall before; the sun is shining so beautifully through those trees, and there are children playing on the corner now. Of course you haven't seen this street before!'

After that session my journey 'back' along Cunningham Place was quite an exercise in awareness.

*

She was more interested in the actuality of the person in her room than she was in theoretical constructions. In her efforts to reach this actuality, she would tell endless stories about herself, or from novels and plays, fairy tales and mythology.

83

She conversed with those who visited her as one would a friend, though with a steadier undercurrent of instruction and exhortation.

She told me of a time in her childhood when she was locked in her room for disobedience. Her mother was entertaining some friends at tea. Buntie stuffed a pair of stockings and dangled them down past the sitting-room window. The ladies rushed up to her room in alarm. When they opened the door, Buntie slipped past them and ran out. She stayed away for the rest of the day. After that, her mother did not try to punish her, but would talk to her about her misdeeds.

Why did she tell me these stories? Part of it was friendship: to build a connection, to share things. But there was an exemplary dimension, too. Usually one felt her stories had some direct bearing on one's own situation, but she would never say directly what it was. She had been a lively child who lived fully the free-spirited energy of childhood. She would tell me about how her mother used to let her run around in shorts, very unusual in those days, and go climbing with her older brother. She was not ashamed of her acts of disobedience. They had been good mischievous fun, and they had got her mother to acknowledge her point of view.

When in her early 'teens she had refused to be confirmed in the Scottish Presbyterian Church, her father was so furious that he struck her, but her mother defended her and she won the argument. I think Buntie saw how tortured and tangled I could get in my own feelings of guilt and wanted to free me by telling me stories like that.

*

Buntie once told me a story about Teresa of Avila. Saint Teresa seemed to be praying. She heard two young nuns walking past say, 'Oh, Saint Teresa is having a vision.' And Saint Teresa, hearing this, kept her counsel and when they passed, she carried on with her shopping list.

*

I cannot remember now the context of many of Buntie's stories. Even at the time I often did not understand but I always knew that there was some good reason for her to tell a story – though reason is too concrete a word for her subtle intuitive approach. Perhaps she herself could not have explained why the conversation took the course it did.

*

Buntie told me a story about the time she was in Kent during the war and found herself with all the East Enders who went down to Kent for their annual jaunt to pick hops. They were not the sort of people Buntie had much experience with. After a couple of days one large woman came over to where Buntie was standing in the field, lifted up her skirts and proceeded to relieve herself virtually on Buntie's foot. Buntie was only too aware she was being tested. She didn't react at all. She merely walked over to where she was boiling water and asked the woman if she would like a cup of tea. From that moment Buntie was totally accepted. 'It was an important moment for me because my instinctive function was not strong,' she said.

*

Buntie felt dignity in a woman was so important. I cannot remember how many times she told me the story of the mistress of a famous author who was in a German concentration camp during the war. The women were ordered

85

to line up for the roll call. The commandant started to approach this woman for some reason I cannot remember now. As he raised his whip to her, she, gaunt, having little of her physical beauty left, reached out, grabbed the whip, and broke it over her knee, never once taking her eyes from his face. As Buntie told the story, he did not touch her.

*

At one point in my lessons Buntie kept telling me the story of someone she knew. She must have told me the story several times until one day, having finished the story, she looked at me and took my hands in hers. I knew too that I had finally understood not from my head but from my heart. This is the story:

This man, who was a soldier, elderly now and quite dignified, used to walk to the local newsagent every day for a newspaper. He used a walking stick as he was slightly disabled. One day he was approached by a young man who menacingly demanded his wallet. Without saying a word this elderly gentleman took out his wallet and threw it on the ground. When the young man bent over to pick it up, he hit him with the stick – enough merely to stun him. The elderly man then bent down, picked up his wallet, and proceeded on his way.

For me, this story was to do with having the courage of my convictions.

*

One December Buntie told me a story. A Roman Catholic priest had arrived at his church very early on Christmas morning to prepare for Mass. To his great consternation the figure of the Christ Child was missing from the crib. Just then he heard an unusual noise approaching up the aisle and withdrew behind a pillar to observe what it was.

Trundling towards him was a little child, a member of his flock, pushing a small new wheelbarrow in which lurched the missing Baby Jesus. Reaching the crib, with great concentration and some considerable difficulty the boy replaced the figure where he belonged. 'There!' the priest heard him say, 'I told you if I got one you'd be the first to ride in it.'

*

I used to get so impatient when she repeated stories. I can remember thinking, 'She's getting past it.' She would see the look on my face and say, 'Look now, I'm telling you this story for a point.'

A friend of mine had the same experience. Only she finally recognised what was happening and said to Buntie, 'Once I've understood it, you don't tell me the same story any more, do you?!'

*

It was a bad sign when, three times running, Buntie summarised for me the plot of Hedda Gabler, the story of a beautiful and talented woman whose identification with her father leaves her inflamed with unfocussed ambition, obsessed with a longing to dominate, and in the end, murderously destructive. She must have felt that I myself showed some signs of being overtaken by a power-mad animus. There was a nameless woman Buntie kept bringing up, 'very gentle and feminine, but her animus was a thug. A real thug!' Once, commenting on my mother's tendency to live a life of rules and obligations, of 'should,' 'ought,' and moral emphasis, Buntie said, 'Your mother's animus has her under lock and key. Under lock and key!'

After my three sessions with Hedda Gabler, Buntie told me the story of the Snow Queen, where the sister's quest for her brother is also a struggle to join the masculine and feminine aspects of the psyche. The robber-girl who helps the sister is an example of a woman whose comfortable relation with her animus (she lives at ease among the robbers) enables her to act with bold resolution and clarity, and with unsentimental generosity.

*

Again and again – and again – she told me this story about a little girl who had no friends, no toys. All that she had to do was go round and round and round in a yard. Most times I would think, 'Oh, here we go again.' One day the story touched me and I finally cried. Buntie said, 'Good, my sweetheart, you're showing compassion.'

*

We must be absent for awareness to be present.

THE WORK

The therapeutic process consisted largely of a great deal of hard work, learning to understand in new ways and changing old attitudes. With Buntie this centred on relationships, dreams and 'homework.'

*

Relationships

Buntie regarded relationship, both inner and outer, as a major part of the work. What were often presented as problems with relationships, she saw as opportunities for growth. With regard to her own relationship with her pupils, she averred that it was the same as any other, two individuals meeting on terms acceptable to both parties at all times and learning to know each other in increasing depth.

*

The only time I saw Buntie I was in such distress that a friend had 'loaned' me her session. When I sat down Buntie said,'What's the problem?'

'I can't cope,' I said.

She looked me full in the eye and said, 'But who wants to cope and, more importantly, who wants to be coped with? If you were a child, would you want to be coped with?'

I cannot even count the number of friends with children with whom I have shared this in the years since – or how many times I have repeated it to myself. As I move 'managing' my family to 'professional' managing,' the challenge remains fresh in its significance.

*

Among the few Jungian terms that Buntie used frequently were 'anima,' referring to the feminine element in the male psyche, and 'animus,' referring to the masculine element in the female psyche. She felt it important to make a good 'inner marriage' with the opposing presence of masculine or feminine in the psyche, learning to release and value its positive energy without getting caught in its negative aspect. Several years earlier, on the London stage, there had been a play she loved to talk about. It had four characters: a man, his wife, the houri who embodied the sentimental, indulgently seductive anima of the man, and the knight who embodied the self-righteous, indulgently ennobled animus of the woman. The wife could see all the fantastic daydreams in her husband's anima, but not in her own animus, while her husband could see all that was unrealistic and vain in her animus, but not in his own anima. After some indignant clashes, both husband and wife came to see how longings and fantasies shaped their view of things. Only then could they arrive at a more creative interplay between masculine and feminine, with their differing modes of perception and response, their differing sets of values.

*

Over 30 years ago, but I can remember it like yesterday, I ran into her in Hamilton Terrace while I was airing two dogs, and I spoke to her about a friend of mine, whom she also knew, who was in a big dilemma over her man, and she said, 'Until the male becomes conscious of the positive feminine within himself, most women have to find their independence from the masculine within them and live by their own active positive feminine.'

*

When Buntie and I were discussing the men in my life she said, 'Don't let them ride their tricycles all over your garden. Make them keep to the pathways.'

*

If things were heavy with my relationship, as they usually were, and I felt there was no way of resolving it, Buntie would just look at me and say, 'Get him out of your head. Don't keep him rattling around and around in circles, just get him out of your head and pull him, dearest, into your heart.'

'Keep him in your heart,' she would repeat as she motioned with her hands the movement from head to heart.

*

I was having a terrible, painful time in my partnership. Buntie and I must have discussed this relationship every session for years. One time when the impasse seemed so great and my inability to let go equally great, she went underneath it all, in that way she had, and said, 'Trust. Just trust.'

'But I don't trust him,' I admitted ruefully.

'No, my sweetheart, trust in life.'

I have to laugh now at her gift of the simple phrase and the tall order.

91

*

One time we were talking about communicating love to one's partner. She said, 'There is no need to say anything. Just have loving feelings towards him. He will pick them up, don't worry.'

She felt it was essential to keep love fresh and alive and strongly believed that a couple should not live in each other's pockets. She would say that it was essential to have space and movement and separation and one's own interests and friends as well as joint ones. She said that otherwise, the relationship would become stale.

After I got married she said that we would go together to a garden centre by the canal near her and that she would buy us a pink rose and a white rose which when planted would grow up and twine together, this being a representation of the masculine and feminine energies. I was very touched by her thought. Unfortunately we never managed it for various practical reasons. But I still intend to plant the roses, partly now as a remembrance of her love and spirit.

*

Buntie was the first person I could ever remember who *recognized* me. It was years after this first meeting that I realised this was what had made me feel so comfortable and right in our sessions. Once I described a feeling I was yearning to receive from the man I was living with. She said that feeling is recognition – or, as she put it, re-cognition. 'How,' she aske, 'could anybody recognize you when you have not yet re-cognized yourself?'

*

92

Buntie once wrote to me: 'Failures and difficulties in relationship are a failure to love. It is not that the other is failing us in not loving us enough but that we are failing to love them enough to put our own interest second. As soon as we say, "I must possess it/him/her" and that is projected, misery will begin. Serve life in whatever way it presents itself and life will serve you – in this lies happiness and calmness and peaceful work, conscientiously carried out without motive. The calmer we are and the less disturbed our nerves, the more we shall love and the better will be our work.'

*

Buntie sent me a letter after seeing both myself and the man I was living with in the same session: 'These notes might help for homework! I love you both and would like to help you resolve if not totally solve your dilemmas over the relationship. Blessing, Buntie.'

*

Buntie talked to me about love. 'It is in the moments when you are really there (when the self rises to the surface past the ego), when no projections, demands, or longings block your view, when you are dwelling clearly in the present moment, then what you feel is love.'

To me, with my cravings for romance, that was a revelation. Love was not, then, a passionate upwelling of devotion or desire, but a readiness for connection that could come as naturally as breathing. She had a concept of 'meeting' that fits with this. 'Meeting, which happens too rarely, comes when two people are both fully present, seeing and responding to one another without distortion.'

*

93

With one sentence she could lift a burden that had troubled one for years. All my life I had worried about the health of my parents. One day she said to me: 'Stop worrying about the bodies of your mother and father. If they are happy in their spirits they are all right.'

*

She once told me, having listened yet again to my upset outpourings about the way my father treated my mother: 'Say to him, in a quiet but firm way, that it really distresses you hearing him speak in such a derogatory way because it reflects so badly on himself, not your mother.' It took me years to pluck up the courage to do so, but one day the opportunity did arise, and it was amazing how effective the words were.

*

Buntie understood relationships, particularly those difficult father-son, mother-daughter relationships which defeat so many of us. She believed that it was important that a son knew what his father did so that the father's work away from home had a reality. One day the window cleaner at Cunningham Place asked Buntie for her advice about his son about whom he was anxious for some reason. Buntie suggested that he take his son with him on some of his rounds. This he did and immediately found that the relationship improved.

*

On the subject of raising children Buntie was clear and to the point: 'Remember the most important thing of all is to give them as little to carry as possible.'

*

Buntie was quite willing to work with more than one person from the same family, a husband and wife, a mother and daughter, as long as they themselves wanted and could accept the arrangement. They would meet in individual sessions, only rarely as groups. 'Because, you see,' said Buntie, 'I can look from each point of view. I don't take sides, I think about what each person needs.'

She wanted to meet both my daughter and my husband. (My Freudian analyst, by contrast, thought that, on the whole, meeting anyone intimately connected with me would be 'inappropriate to our work together.') She arranged to have one session with my husband, so that they could 'get acquainted.' She also invited me to bring my three-year-old daughter to have tea with her. Afterwards, she told me that my daughter was good with her hands (she'd had blocks and crayons to play with) and had the facial expressions of a natural comedienne. She wanted me to see that it is important for parents to 'recognize' their children, so seeing what their natural gifts and inclinations are and offering ways of pursuing them.

Buntie also arranged for me to have one session jointly with my husband. I sat in my usual seat; my husband sat behind me, off to one side and further back. 'I always give the wives the centre seat,' said Buntie mischievously. 'The husbands don't like it. They are used to being more important.' She asked each of us to talk about what first drew us to each other and then to talk abut what each of us most needed from the other. Those apparently simple questions stirred up a surprising number of feelings that usually lay dormant.

*

95

During one summer while Buntie was on holiday I had got involved with someone. I described what a relief it was to meet a caring man and of course it wasn't serious, he was married. I will always feel her response: 'My sweetheart, whenever we get involved with someone, we have no idea where life will take us. But,' she added, in recognition of my star-crossed history in relationships, 'I will help you to see this one through.'

At the height – or depth? – of our difficulties about our relationship and his marriage, my lover agreed to go to see Buntie. If I am honest, I will have to admit that part of me expected her to brandish a magic wand and presto! it would all work out. In retrospect I was glad Buntie had seen him; I think it helped her to help me stay grounded in the realities of our difficulties.

I am also glad of the lesson I learned about the magic wand. There was no easy way out, only living through what this deep connection meant for me. I felt that we talked about the relationship every session for years. But, as she said more than once to me, 'You are in exactly the place you need to be to learn the lessons you need to learn at the present time.'

Some old patterns kept reappearing and jeopardizing my relationships. Because of her love, support and, yes, professional skill, I was (very slowly) able to recognize that I had some things to live out, work through, heal – and that 'changing men' was neither here nor there. I learned that in making a better relationship with myself, I would be better able to make a relationship with someone else – whether it was this man (as it has turned out, to our surprise) or someone else.

She often recommended Irene Claremont de Castillejo's *Knowing Woman*, and the bit in it that struck me most forcefully was her point that the most important thing is not to 'work on' the relationship, but to look to yourself.

*

There was an occasion when I was in a terrible state because my boyfriend had gone off with another woman. Buntie said gently, 'Well dearest, I remember that you too have gone off with another woman's husband.' It put things in a much clearer, and more honest perspective.

*

I would be telling Buntie about something awful someone had said to me, and then how I reacted, and on and on, with great indignation and self-righteousness or hurt. Sometimes at the end of such a tale, Buntie would not say anything. She would just toss the case for her glasses on to the floor in front of her.

The first time this happened, I instinctively reached to pick it up.

'No, just leave it. It is theirs. But the minute you pick it up, it becomes yours. Just leave it, my sweetheart. Then eventually they will have to bend down and pick it up themselves.'

*

Raging and storming at a particularly difficult point in my life, continually asking Buntie 'why' but never listening for the answer, I was finally told, 'You'll never understand why until you pick up responsibility for your own part in things.'

*

I was convinced that my second-in-command was useless and I needed to change his behaviour. He was in charge of the coffee bar in our centre for teenagers yet never managed to get new mugs when some broke or to bring in clean tea towels on schedule. I talked about him session after session, how he never did this or that. I had really got obsessed about him: those tea towels became the first thing I looked for when I came in to work.

Finally Buntie said to me, 'My sweetheart, what does your desk look like?' I had to admit that my desk made the tea towels look clean, of course.

Then she said, 'If you will attend to your own desk and get into relationship with that, you'll be surprised what happens with him.'

That was one of those encounters that shifted my perception immediately – immediately after months, I mean. It finally sank in that the only person I could do something about was me, that perhaps I should get on with attending to my own mess and see what happens.

*

Buntie would enunciate the simplest, most easily forgotten truths about life. I would think, 'Oh yes, this is obvious,' then realize how feebly I'd understood it till then.

'Do you know what friendship is?' she asked me. I was silent, overwhelmed by my sense of the complexity of all my friendships, with fears, distrust, rivalry, hostility surging unconfronted beneath the surface.

'Friendship is sharing,' she said (meaning not pieces of pie, but concerns, interests, perceptions). I suddenly felt a marvellous sense of release, with all my usual psychic murk not so much denied as by-passed.

*

I used to get in a great tizz about not seeing friends; I work really hard and I felt such pressure and such guilt when I did not see friends regularly. 'Dearest,' she said, 'Never see someone because you ought or should, only when you feel moved to do so. Otherwise, there will be nothing in depth in the meeting. Filling up your time will also mean that when someone truly needs you, in depth, you will have no space for them, neither inner nor outer.'

*

*The healing light of the sun enables us to see
the colours of the brethren and to understand their very nature.*

*

Dreams

Dreams provided a rich source of material for work. Buntie, with her Jungian background, was skilled at unlocking their messages. She insisted that they be written down and sent or brought to her. Always she wanted a title. After analyzing them, she often sent people away to paint or sculpt them or work them into short plays. She believed they were a rich source of information about a pupil's inner life, bringing things to the surface that the conscious mind may have been blocking but was now ready to face.

*

Sessions usually started, in my case, with the reading of 'homework' I had done, which often included dreams. How is it that one cannot interpret one's own dreams without help? Their significance can seem so obvious, once understood. Buntie did not immediately tell one what was obvious to her: she asked leading questions, and brought out the memories and associations aroused by the symbolism, of which I knew something. Sometimes she would tell me to draw my dreams. This, although I am a trained artist, I never wanted to do or felt capable of doing. But I obeyed and did always manage to produce a fair representation of what I had dreamt. This would lead to further associations of ideas, with fruitful results. Gradually we uncovered the presence of a strongly negative influence in my early family background of which I was quite unaware, though conscious of other difficulties. Yet I had dreamt of this constantly.

*

Buntie had a dream. In the dream she was sitting before her teacher Toni Sussman and Toni was knitting, as she often did when you went to see her. Above Toni's head appeared this practically naked man, dressed only in a loincloth, sitting cross-legged over her head.

Buntie recounted her dream to Toni in her next session. Toni looked up from the knitting, seized a book from the bookshelf, opened it at a picture, held it out and said, 'Is this the man?' And it was. Buntie said, 'Yes! Who is it?' Toni closed the book with a bang, shoved it back on the shelf, and said, 'Not yet.'

'Not yet' was an instruction that did not go well with Buntie's temperament and she was determined to find out who this man was. She went down to John Watkins' bookshop and spoke to him about it, then went through every book with sages and gurus on the shelves, everybody it could possibly have been. It took hours and she didn't find anything. So Buntie finally admitted that possibly 'not yet' was the case. As she was leaving the shop, there was a little wire rack with pamphlets loosely scattered in it, things on offer for a few pence. One caught her eye: it was completely plain on the cover except for the question in print: WHO AM I? She opened it up and there was a photo of Sri Ramana Maharshi, and that is how Buntie's relationship to Ramana, which was to be so central in her life, started. It might encourage the rest of us that she never had the courage to tell Toni what she had done.

*

Buntie told me how as a child she had dreams of being in a strange country and drinking a tea which was salty, sour and buttery. There were men with funny hats. Only when she was an adult did she recognise these dreams as being situated in Tibet. She had not seen photos or been told about the tea as a child, so she felt that these dreams must be some kind of memory from a previous incarnation.

At the time I had hardly heard of reincarnation, much less decided whether I believed in it or not. But by sharing her own experience Buntie – whose integrity I trusted so implicitly – gave me an opportunity to consider things that were at that time beyond my conscious grasp.

*

I remember some of Buntie's dream admonitions well:

'Next time you dream of that baby, you will please remember to take care of it.'

'Next time you dream of that beautiful young boy offering to make love to you – say Yes!'

'Next time you dream of finding a handbag with all sorts of wonderful things inside, don't give it back, keep it! Your handbag is your femininity.'

*

When I was no longer ill and in such desperate need of help, I continued to see Buntie, first regularly, then occasionally for the next few years. It was during this period that a major turning point came to me through a dream. (There were many others of less importance.) I was then working as a draughtsman in an oil company, where I had a room to myself. I was happy in my work. I dreamed that I got to the office late, and not properly dressed. I had some better

101

clothes with me and wanted to put them on, but could not because at the back of the room there was a man standing, silently painting me at an easel. He wouldn't go away. The turning point was the realization which Buntie had to push me into, that my job, which I liked, was not all I wanted in life. The artist-animus would not go away, and because of him I could not be wholly satisfied with my office life. This realization was indeed painful: I wept on the top of a bus, going home afterwards. I had been evading responsibility, not wanting to know that I had to be an artist.

*

On my birthday Buntie sent me a card with a bird on the front, a beautiful Far Eastern painting. She told me afterwards that she saw me somehow as a little bird. Funnily enough, when I was very ill with viral pneumonia sometime after, I had a very vivid dream of a bird which came to my chest and lightly pecked at me. It was a healing and releasing dream, and the next day I felt a lot better.

*

Moments of perfect happiness have most often come in dreams Occasionally, though with less absolute completeness, I have also experienced real happiness in actual life.

The first such dream was when I was about 14. It was just a clearing in a wood with a slightly scorched patch where a small fire had been. That was all, but it is linked with another moment on a rain-wet road. The road was on a bend with tall hedges and long wet grass, and I felt the slight chill of the rain. Both were my first flashes of perfect happiness in dreams and have remained with me always.

The second dream was when I was about 16. Again it was only a flash – like the uncovering for a moment of some lovely secret. It was of a tree in blossom and it extended across the whole of my vision so that there wasn't room for anything else on the 'canvas.' It filled me with ecstasy for years after.

One 'live' experience of utter happiness was when I was about 21 and with some friends in a tiny pub garden in Gloucestershire. There was a swing and I sat on it and as it went up I had a view over hollyhocks, sweet peas and other bright crowded flowers, surrounded by hills.

When I used to experience these 'live' moments I was also filled with a kind of despair, because I wanted to 'be' what I was experiencing. However, I seemed always outside, never a part of these happenings.

'I want to be *it*,' I explained once to Buntie, with regret. All she replied was: ' . . . but you are *it*!'

Immediately I felt as if a key had unlocked a door. Now the feeling of sadness has been replaced by joy that I am part of *it* and *it* is part of me.

*

Once I had a dream with my husband in it, and I was thinking, 'That's my husband doing so and so. I'd better watch out for that.' And Buntie reminded me, 'That's you. It's your dream.' She always pushed you back to what that person in the dream represented inside you.

*

A couple of times I had dreams which were not like the other dreams. They were more three-dimensional, as if I were genuinely meeting the person in the dream – one time my grandmother, another a former lover. 'Of course my sweetheart, you did meet them,' Buntie commented quite matter-of-factly. For me it was such a relief that healing meetings could take place 'in the spirit' if not the flesh.

*

I remember once at the beginning of my time with Buntie, I dreamed of a miniature cow standing on the cooker in my kitchen. Buntie, with that wry and wicked sense of humour that was nevertheless so kind, responded: 'Congratulations. I'm delighted you've managed to produce something resembling female maternity, no matter how tiny.' For a career woman who had shied away from motherhood and domesticity of all kinds, it was indeed an achievement!

*

I had an extremely shocking dream in which the man I was living with dressed-up in a very camp manner, walked into Buntie's room, put her over his knee and spanked her. I told Buntie about it. She asked how I perceived her in real life. 'As a wise, spiritual woman,' I replied. 'Then this man is behaving in this way to that wise and spiritual part of you,' she said. The dream helped reinforce my feelings that my relationship with this man, which was already unsatisfactory, was not healthy and would need to end.

*

Buntie once told me a dream of hers. She was in a room with a Buddhist Lama. It was a long room with windows at one end and a door at the other. He was wearing saffron robes and discussing her work.

He said to her, 'Your job is to keep the windows clean and to help each pupil to find their own particular window – and then to jump through it.'

*

Buntie worked with dreams as much as possible. Even though I either dream very little or remember very little of what I dream, she did find some fragments to use. Once when I had a dream set on the seashore, she said, 'Ah, that's very good. The shore is the edge of the unconscious, you know.'

When I dreamed of a woman who travelled under the sea, releasing children who were tangled in seaweed and rusty chains, she said, 'Yes, she's releasing new life from old habits and outmoded ways of thought, and letting it rise to the surface.'

She was keen on getting people to draw their dreams and once persuaded me to produce a drawing of a fair-haired youth ('puer aeternus,' she announced), riding a bicycle on a little road that wound through gentle, shrub-covered sand dunes. 'And you quite liked doing that, didn't you?' she said. To give me courage (I think my drawings are terrible) she showed me some dream-drawings other 'sweethearts' had made and had given her permission to show. Most of them were no more 'finished,' technically, than my own.

Once I had a dream in which my husband and I were seated at a rectangular table, with a man who had been my lover years before on one side and the woman he was living with on the other. 'What type are you?' asked Buntie, unexpectedly. She was asking, of course, which one of the four functions Jung described as dominant orientations in the human psyche – thought, feeling, instinct, and intuition – held most sway in me? 'I don't know,' I replied, never having been able to figure it out.

'Where were you sitting then?' My husband had been at the head of the table (top of the sheet in the diagram I drew), I at the bottom, my former lover on the left, his lover on the right. Buntie showed me a diagram of the traditional positions of the four functions: thought at the top (north), feeling at the bottom (south), instinct to the left (west), intuition to the right (east). The diagram fitted. Immediately it seemed obvious

105

that my husband was a thinking type, I a feeling type, the other man instinctive and the woman intuitive. It took me a long time to puzzle out what Jung means by feeling, because it is for him a rational function which makes decisions about ethical and emotional values – not the meaning one usually expects. But now when I stumble across Jungian discussions of feeling types, I find that aspects of myself which had always seemed baffling form parts of a coherent pattern with an underlying rationale. This is oddly reassuring.

*

Several times, Buntie told me one of her own dreams. As a young woman, she had had a sharp, often sarcastic tongue and had prided herself on her wit. She had a close relationship with one of the men who helped in her therapeutic training, but sometimes she would attack him in 'play' with her clever, cutting remarks. Then one night she dreamt that a man with a dagger was coming towards her, closer and closer, and stabbed her deep in the chest. 'The heart centre,' she said. 'And when I woke up,' she added, 'I was quite sick. For two weeks. After that, I found my sharp tongue had disappeared. I had to feel it, do you see?'

*

After Buntie's death we received our old 'homework' back, all in order with our names on each batch of papers and paintings. Mine came in a pink folder, tied with a pink ribbon, and for a long time I could not bring myself to open it. When I did I found that as we had worked together on dreams she had underlined the important points she wanted to make. This was usually in red ink and occasionally comments were added, such as 'neglected,' 'feeling tone,' 'negative animus'; these she had explained as we went over the dream.

106

comments were added, such as 'neglected,' 'feeling tone,' 'negative animus'; these she had explained as we went over the dream.

She always asked what I would put as a title and then would write it as a heading in the same red ink. I was often at a loss for a true title, but when I did not try too hard it would often come spontaneously. One which she wrote was 'The power of the Witch is not infinite,' and I am sure that it came from me after describing an old witch with an enormous club in her hands, who was beating the life out of the person I loved while I was an impersonal on-looker. The word 'jealousy' was written in the margin at that point, which was right on the mark! However, in the next scene the loved one was present and perfectly all right.

Buntie also encouraged me to write a scene between the characters in my dream, especially when I had been able to paint the scene first. One I wrote was where the aforesaid husband and myself were in jail together and I was trying to flirt with the jailor to get our release, but he was only interested in another woman for whom he was arranging a private plane to escape. Then I tried to use all my wiles to persuade her to leave our cell windows open and smuggle us on the plane. Unfortunately when this had been arranged the jailor came back delighted that he could accompany her to the frontier so my plans were quashed.

This was the first time I had ever attempted a little fantasy and I was very reluctant to try, but it opened up a new dimension to my writing and to the continuation of the stories in my dreams, and to my power to alter them in a positive way; for example the prison windows could have been left open and we could have escaped from our shackles.

*

What do I especially remember her for? I was touched that she at once sensed (and thereby affirmed) my own poetic sense and feeling for beauty, within and without, about which I have always felt ambivalent. I recall her special emphasis on the puer aeternus – the symbol of freshly burgeoning life within, and on the child – the symbol of wholeness and integration. I recall her refusal to allow me always to begin by doing myself down. Her dream interpretation was itself creative art, encouraging significant images and stories to emerge in one of my most continuously 'dream-creative' phases. I miss that now. What a wonderful and vital language I began to see in dreams. It was very important, in particular, to learn that a regularly recurring dream-figure was my anima, not my enemy: not to be feared or driven out, but to be allowed an important integrating function in my unconscious.

But, perhaps, in the end, there was simply her deep sense, her deep-rooted and confident wisdom, and the feeling that, in the line going back through her to Toni Sussman to Jung himself, the true life of the spirit was in a way making itself known.

*

*In our sleep, pain that cannot forget falls drop by drop
upon the heart and in our despair, against our will
comes wisdom through the awful grace of God.*

Aeschylus

*

Work and Homework

Therapy with Buntie was conducted both within the consulting room and outside, in your daily life. The sessions were for unloading, opening up, discovering and learning. But she also required her pupils to take away what had occurred there and integrate it in the days or weeks that followed. She often gave 'homework' in the form of creative tasks – writing, painting, sculpting – to aid this process. This 'homework,' which she always kept, was sent to her through the post or brought to the next visit.

*

When I went to see Buntie I noticed all these often rough, handmade things on every surface. Once I said, 'What's all this?'

'People's homework,' she said with such reverence.

There was modelling and stones set out in patterns and bits of plasticine and shells. She used to show them with pride. I suspect there was an inner reason for keeping them there, almost alchemy. I certainly know what it meant to me to see the stones I had brought in my first session sitting up there on her mantel with the exquisite Japanese netsuke and the clay models.

There was also the homework we wrote and sent to her or dropped in the door sometime before a session: dreams, thoughts, stories, paintings. Her secretary said she couldn't part with it. Sometimes she would parcel it up and get ready to return it, then she'd say, 'No, keep it a bit longer.' I know she didn't want to keep it for herself but somehow felt the need to keep it safe for us, in trust, until she knew that whatever it was about had resolved.

She did not believe in this three times a week therapy. 'Homework' – doing writing and painting and modelling – was a way people could go and continue their own therapy, for themselves. *You* had to take it out of that room. It was part of how she saw therapy.

This stretched to 'work' as well. It wasn't just writing, it was doing things, putting all this into practice. For me, she mentioned T'ai-Chi repeatedly for years before I finally got round to it, and Bach's rescue remedy for stress, and things to do with my work. And she put me in touch with people who could help me or needed my help. Sometimes these 'introductions' clicked, sometimes not, but I see now her fine skill in helping me to feel special without keeping the whole experience precious to that room.

*

I have strong memories of the 'homework' I did in the little studio I rented while staying in London for my two or three-week visits each year. Buntie would often have me do an active imagination with one of the characters of my dreams. This almost always brought up a wealth of material both painful and joyful. I would then do a painting or more often a series of paintings about this encounter. Some of the paintings I did during those sessions I still have here and I look at them now six or seven years later and find they give me new insights and strengths.

I would take the paintings to Buntie at the next session and we would look at them together. And Buntie would of course affirm the positive parts and help me to see the various aspects of myself in the dreams. The more I did these paintings the bolder the forms and colours became and the bolder the forms and colours became in my dreams; as if Buntie and I were giving my unconscious permission to be really free.

*

110

Buntie said to me once, when I arrived at her place wearing high-heeled shoes, that I had lovely feet and good legs and I should take every opportunity to show them off. She said it quite seriously, as though it should be part of my homework in finding and honouring the feminine that was mine.

*

Once when I was feeling flat and empty and it was, as Buntie put it, winter in my garden, she gave me as homework a mission, an assignment, as I suspect she gave most of us from time to time. This one was perhaps uncommon in psychiatric/psychological circles.

She sent me to Brighton for 24 hours – I'd never been there before – with the sole objective of buying her a vulgar postcard and sending it to her not, she specified, in an envelope, but open through the post, so that her secretary, the postman, etc. etc. etc. would have to read it. And I did. I went off to Brighton, spent 24 hours, rain poured down and the sense of being on a Buntie adventure made it a very sweet 24 hours. And a very useful exercise it proved, possibly because of its apparent futility – but afterwards it wasn't winter in my garden any more.

*

I loved Buntie for her practicality and good sense. I had a new manager of a factory and I was worried about him but never seemed to be able to find time to visit him. The factory was next to my house (my own office was 15 miles away). Buntie said, 'Why don't you get him to start a little earlier and talk to him for 10 minutes every day before you go to work?' So simple, why had I not thought of it?

*

I have just been rereading copies of some of the letters that I wrote to Buntie between our meetings. I believe she saw her task as enabling me to clarify certain things – thoughts about my parents, my partner, my childless state, my work. Initially my 'homework' consisted in relating these thoughts and my experiences. Later, Buntie set me specific topics, e.g. On Being Sensitive, On Love Between Man and Woman, On Fear. Later still, I read books that Buntie recommended and wrote comments for her. The two that impressed me very much and influenced me the most were *The Inner World of Choice* by Frances Wickes and *Knowing Woman* by Irene Claremont de Castillejo.

*

*By accepting what is nearest at hand and
working through it out of love —
man can make himself ready for what will become
in time the greatest journey of all.*

Laurens van der Post

THE UNORTHODOX THERAPIST

Among Buntie's many qualities as a therapist, arguably her most distinctive was her active involvement with those who came to see her. She was unusual in that she 'transgressed' many of the rules of therapeutic practice. It seemed to work. But 'unorthodox' never meant 'unprofessional.'

*

It has always been very difficult to explain to people what Buntie was, because no label ever fitted. In fact, she taught me the enormous, crucial importance of not labelling myself or anyone else or anything.

*

Buntie once came to a party I had years go – I think it was the only time she ever came to my house. She came for half an hour or so. Later on somebody said to me, 'Who was that extraordinary woman who seemed to be so wise?' And I said, 'Tell me a bit more.'

And this young girl said, 'I asked her what she did and she said that she wore out an armchair in St. Johns Wood.'

*

She once said to me, with disdain: 'Some therapists are told they are not meant to have any physical contact with their clients. I think that's a load of rubbish.' She similarly dismissed the usual 'professional' notion of having ten minutes break between clients to recover one's centre. For her it wasn't necessary, she explained. Buntie taught by 'touching' the deep core within.

And so I learnt what it was to have an open heart, to trust, to be intimate without losing or compromising any part of yourself. For, in spite of all her giving, Buntie never lost her dignity, authority, or integrity, for one second. She was paradoxically the ultimate professional.

Similarly I learned by the environment Buntie created about her. Gradually I understood something about the importance of the Feminine – a constant theme of Buntie's work–by the pictures on her walls of the Madonna and child, by the flowers that stood on her mantelpiece, by her treasuring of the pieces of 'homework' in clay or shells or paint that graced her shelves. The gentle, creative, nourishing aspects of life that are so neglected, and worse, abused in our harsh times. Over the years that I visited Buntie these images seeped into my own consciousness, backing up her words, until I too began to feel their vital importance, and the honour that is due to them.

Her large chest of drawers next to where she sat was also a potent teaching aid. Always the top of the chest represented the edge between the conscious and the unconscious – the drawers below representing the murky depths of shadow and less aware levels of mind. I can never see that bit of furniture without remembering the levels above and below the 'pavement' as Buntie used to call it.

I once asked her if she was ever lonely – if she ever regretted not having children. 'I treasure my time alone,' she replied. 'And you, the sweethearts, are all my family.'

114

*

Whenever you finally 'saw the point,' reached a new understanding, a new level of awareness, the handclasp she then gave you was welcoming, as to a fellow-traveller journeying on the same path.

*

She was also, I came to realise, quite unorthodox. She was as concerned to help me find a remedy for my migraine attacks via homeopathy, diet or whatever, as to help me explore my feelings and relationships. She would not hesitate to put an arm around me or hold my hand when she knew I needed that and I was always aware, both that I was special for the hour I spent with her, and also that I was neither more nor less special than the person who had come before or the one who would come after. There was something immensely reassuring about this.

*

On account of her Scottish origins physical contact ('touch') did not come easily to Buntie, and yet more and more did it become manifest latterly as she increasingly frequently hugged her 'sweethearts.' That touch was a vital part of her teaching and her healing.

Being myself Scottish, Buntie spent quite a lot of time trying to help me with the same difficulty. On several occasions, she gave me a lively, vivid and amusing mime of her own mother's reactions to her efforts at trying to embrace her. It was a mime of a person trying to chase away from her face and head a swarm of particularly noxious and disagreeable insects.

*

I can give one practical example of how Buntie 'worked alongside me.' At the convent grammar school where I taught, I was asked by the headmistress to produce a play, preferably Shakespeare, at the end of the summer term. The Lent term when we began reading *The Merchant of Venice* was a time of conflict and confusion in other areas of my life and although the girls were enthusiastic and in some cases talented, the stage itself was a horrendous problem. I poured out to Buntie my fears and frustrations: she wanted facts, figures and measurements. I gave her details of the polished floor (therefore no nails or screws to support the scenery), the polished wooden choir stalls in a three-tiered semicircle at the back, the immaculate newly painted cream walls, grand new grey curtains which would not be in place until the week of the dress rehearsal . . . and on and on . . . .

Three days later Buntie handed me a slip of paper. She suggested I telephone the young man, a very good artist who might have a little time to spare. Within two days (by now it was mid-June) he had seen the hall and grasped the problem. Very soon he produced enchanting sketches, met the cast and impressed the powers-that-be of his suitability. Now we knew that Venice could come to NW1. The miracle began to show itself in all sorts of ways. Rehearsals went as never before, musicians practised, costume makers' needles flashed and a professional painter, assisted by ever more willing helpers, worked at his transforming magic.

At last we were able to present an excellent play with some breathtaking scenery. Everyone was delighted; we had achieved more than we had dreamed of. All this was thanks to Buntie who came to an evening performance, arriving early enough to glean more local gossip than I could ever have heard.

Beloved, unforgettable Buntie, thank you.

*

I made an appointment to see Buntie, at the introduction of a friend, when I was three months pregnant and uncertain how/whether to proceed, as I was not married and was considering an abortion.

By the time of the appointment I had already made up my own mind to continue with the pregnancy and face the problems later. Had I not done so, I feel sure that Buntie would have given me the support and courage I was going to need. As it was, the decision made after minimum of discussion, she folded me in her arms and gave me a big hug. Later, she was to send me some flowers in hospital: red roses, with thorns of course!

Looking back on the episode, she did not strike me as a demonstrative person, but she certainly knew how much I needed that hug.

*

At some point in 'my time' with Buntie she told me that what I needed to do was to have a baby. This was quite a shock as I'd never felt any yearnings for motherhood and had also recently been told that for medical reasons I would probably never have children.

Six months later I felt so ill I thought I was dying, only to be told by a doctor I was pregnant. Suddenly and unexpectedly I was elated. I made an appointment to see Buntie whom I hadn't seen for months. I didn't need to tell her, somehow she knew. She put her arms around me and said she was talking to two of us! She was delighted and came to see our daughter soon after she was born. We were thrilled and honoured as it took so much of her time. I am so pleased they both met.

*

From our very first contact, Buntie acknowledged the indivisibility of me the person and me the artist (singer and sometime songwriter). The first time we spoke was on the telephone back in January 1977 and I remember clearly to this day Buntie saying, 'I was given one of your records for Christmas and I enjoyed it very much but I can really hear you singing a different kind of song.' I remember thinking at the time that I was sure she was right but I had no idea just what that 'different song' would sound like.

What Buntie helped me grow over the eight years I worked with her is much more than songs, but it is as if the songs I wrote over that period chart and almost act as a metaphor for many of the other changes. She helped me not to feel apologetic or inferior because what I did both as a singer and a runner of voice workshops was 'simple,' didn't rely on technique or technology, and therefore provided the possibility of directness and intimacy. In this world filled with experts, synthesizers, and success based on size of record sales, it's easy to see how someone who has no formal vocal or musical training can feel inadequate. The one Buntie statement that helped begin changing this for me was, 'Your great strength, my sweetheart, lies in the courage you have to be simple.' And this affirmation is still a great source of the strength that keeps me to my path.

*

Buntie did a lot of her healing and teaching through intuition, as much as through Jungian principles. A friend of mine wanted to see her and spent a long time telling her own life story.

Buntie said to her, 'You'll be a psychotherapist.'

She knew. This seems very miraculous to those of us who do not know what intuition is.

*

A remarkable thing happened in that first session with Buntie, perhaps the most remarkable thing in all the times I saw her. Before I left, she gave me a long look and said, 'You're a writer. Anyone can see that. That's the problem you've been having. You must write.' But I wasn't a writer, not in practice. I was a teacher of English at a small liberal-arts college. My most extensive manuscripts apart from a couple of routine scholarly articles, were comments on student papers. Years earlier, in high school, I had thought I might be a writer. But even then, I'd formed the habit of 'waiting' to write until my studies for school were finished. Learning from my mother's puritan values, I always told myself that writing was 'extra.' Though I longed to do it, I felt I could turn to it only when my 'real work' – tasks assigned by others – was finished . . . .

Of course, the eighty pages of autobiographical manuscript I had written for her must have given her a clue. But I was struck by the positivity of her statement, its confident absoluteness. Not that I was a would-be writer. Not that I was a professor who could sort of write. Buntie understood immediately how incompatible, at least for me, the two ways of living really were. I was not by nature an academician. I was a writer for sure. I felt so *recognized* . . . . It was her unwavering assurance, even when I said, testing her, 'Buntie, how can I be a writer if . . . ?' that gave me the courage to tell myself at last that I must stop trying to adjust myself more effectively to the academic way of life. I must be, alas, a slow and cautious character, because the changes in my life have so far been subtle and few. Their direction, though, is unmistakable. I am going towards what I want to go towards.

*

I was worrying about what I would do when I had to retire from training teachers. 'You will write a book, dearest; it will be quite simple and lovely.' And I have.

*

I had been stuck for weeks with my painting. It was summer time, the garden was in all its splendour, everything invited the creative flow – but stuck I was. The paper – Japanese – was prepared, the colours mixed, the brushes ready, but nothing – energy and imagination had evaporated.

Buntie came round on one of her visits, so long moans to her, with me saying that, for artistic creation, intuition, waiting for inspiration, the creative centre to awaken – one can't just take the bull by the horns.

'Oh yes you can,' Buntie said. 'I have to take the bull by the horns every minute of the day.' And as she was leaving, she acted it all out – arms swinging in the mews outside my little house, saying, 'If you don't take the bull by the horns, it will toss you here, there, and everywhere.'

The next day I started to paint – and painted all summer non-stop, one of my very best summer collections.

*

Buntie was an interventionist. Her therapy was a therapy of engagement. She was full of suggestions, questions, stories, instructions, exhortations. She had no use for the formal and somewhat distant boundaries that so often define relations between therapist and patient, and yet one never felt one knew the private Buntie. Somehow she kept the kind of reserve which is essential to effective therapy, but also had an immediate, spontaneous, playful presence that didn't bother about proper procedures. Once, when I was preceding her up the stairs, she grabbed the belt of my raincoat. 'I'm getting old now, you know,' she laughed. 'I thought you might just as well pull me.'

*

Buntie said to me early on that: 'It is impossible, really, to read more than one paragraph of teaching with less than half (I think she said) a day of study and attention. If you can manage that, you are already doing more than well.'

*

When I bought a house which had a lovely garden, Buntie was most interested, tending gardens being particularly good for developing the female function! She specifically wanted to buy me a red and a white rose to plant in it – representing I believe the union between man and woman, but she became ill and couldn't get round to it. I wonder how many other therapists would buy rose plants as part of the therapy.

*

I was ill in hospital six or so years ago now and Buntie sent me a card with roses on, which was forwarded from my home address. It said that as she didn't know in which hospital I was, this was the only way she could send me roses.

*

I always treasured those post cards, written in different coloured ink, and always signed, *Blessings x Buntie.*

*

After a rough session Buntie put me to 'rest' in cushions in the 'Big Room' (Studio E), with the instruction that I was to ring her at precisely 7.45 a.m. the next morning. I then realised how many others must have been asked to 'check in' with her: a lifeline.

*

Buying my own flat was a turning point for me. It was a new adventure, a wonderful freedom – and terrifying. I wasn't so aware of how terrified I felt as Buntie was. She told me how to ring her at certain times each day in those awful and exciting weeks of settling in. I felt apologetic with each call, but she never sounded anything other than present with my distress. Just that brief connection helped me to centre enough to get through the day.

I know that I was not the only one phoning, by any means. And that she always found time for her own meditation every morning.

*

I often had the last appointment on a Tuesday evening and would stop at the Greek delicatessen in Camden Town on my way to her, buying something for my own supper later, and often some hummus, pitta bread, and olives for Buntie. I knew it wasn't necessary – but I also knew that she often did not even get downstairs for the vegetarian cheese I would see in the fridge, or the homemade soups that other sweethearts sometimes brought. In fact, sometimes the mould that grew on them was disgusting!

Her life revolved around her work. For a long time I thought that her model of being 'on call' virtually 24 hours a day, was the only right way to live if you are committed to your work. Finally, when a love affair demanded some of my 'committed-to-work' time, I had to reconsider this assumption. Looking at the hours she put in and the numbers of us who were so much in her life, I laughingly accused her of being a terrible role model.

I realized that I was confusing a style of life that was right for her, with commitment to a life centred in the spirit. After all, she had once admonished a friend of mine who had young children and would shut them out several times a day so she could meditate, that at this time, her children were her meditation.

And I was also confusing my own stage of the journey: she early on said, 'You will have this same energy later, my sweetheart, but now, with the work we are doing together, you will not.'

*

Buntie was a great believer in homeopathy and osteopathy. Once when I was feeling glum, she dropped some Bach Rescue Remedy on my tongue. Within a few hours I had perked up to the point of giddiness. Another time, telling me I was melancholy too much of the time, she recommended her homeopathic doctor to me. After weeks of delay, I finally went to see her.

Buntie also felt my droopy spirits could have nutritional causes. 'You must take a vitamin-B complex tablet every day!' she said, producing a jar for me. 'Our foods are so processed now. They simply don't nourish us enough.' Consulting a book on nutrition which seemed (I never saw it, so I can't be sure) to combine homeopathy with astrology, she announced that given my birthdate, I was likely to be deficient in calcium and phosphorus. She recommended I eat bran, cabbage, spinach, lettuce, rhubarb, onions, oranges, lemon, limes, nuts, barley, peas, beans, oats. She made me write down the list.

She gave me the name of her osteopath. She must have kept worrying about my curving neck and upper back. I never took this suggestion, but a couple of years later, when I had a wickedly pinched nerve, I saw an osteopath closer to home, in New England. Since that one visit, my posture has improved, my back is more flexible, and the pinched nerve has disappeared.

*

Buntie was so open about herself, in one sense. I was always concerned about my habit of hoarding and not being able to let go of any possessions. Buntie would say, 'Just sort out a little at a time: just one drawer or cupboard,' and she added, 'They always laugh at me as I'm always tidying up as I go.'

*

That balance was always there: the absolute seriousness of the work and the sense of humour in its playfulness as well.

*

Buntie was very unconventional about fees. I remember once when I spent the whole of one session with her talking about my meeting with the Dalai Lama, she absolutely refused payment. 'Telling me about the Dalai Lama has been a gift to me,' she insisted. At other times when financially things were lean she'd either not take money or reduce the fee by half. This attitude towards money only served to indicate further that Buntie was in the caring profession not the psychotherapeutic one.

*

God hugs you.
You are encircled by the arms of the mystery of God.

Hildegard of Bingen

THE TEACHER

Buntie's role as a therapist was, at another level, that of a Teacher. She offered wisdom, a sense of the numinous and a spirituality which out of her own life experience she knew to be the ultimate solution to the problem of human existence. She sowed seeds of thought and understanding and left it to life itself to bring about their germination.

*

The greatest thing was her spirituality and we caught it from her. However she worked with each of us, and whatever we were, I am sure the essence of her work was to stretch us to that level.

*

Buntie was truly a spiritual person in that for her the spirit was reality, and material things – including food and money – secondary irrelevances. And yet if she had simply been what she indeed was, a truly good person living several planes above the rest of us, few of us would have been able to relate to her and she could not have done the good she did.

It was her practicality and down-to-earthness, her sense of righteous anger and her sense of humour that I remember best. To me she was a saint and I take her spirituality, the result of years of the most disciplined self-development, entirely for granted.

*

Like all great teachers Buntie taught by her very being as much as her words. (In fact often what she said made very little sense to me at the time of speaking, clouded as it was in the mystifying depths of Jungian phraseology and symbolism.) But always when I left her it was with a heart made lighter by the feeling that to become Whole was indeed a possibility. So it seemed that the alchemical transformation that invariably happened within that small, fascinating room was achieved because of what Buntie herself had integrated and become from her long, sometimes arduous, always courageous journey into the Self. I think that was for me her greatest gift.

She once said to me, 'There would be no need for people like me (i.e. psychotherapists), if we all listened, really listened to each other.'

*

Being a Geminian, which I suppose is just a way of excusing it, I've always felt drawn in two directions – one of material pleasures, pleasure of physical things, and the other, a very strong spiritual impulse. Coming from my background and education I felt there was a conflict between the two.

One day I spoke of it to Buntie. I told her that I felt almost externally pulled in two different directions and by other people, I myself unsure really which direction was mine.

127

Buntie asked me, in depth which was it my heart was committed to, and I had to answer, of course, the spiritual as the only one that really mattered.

Then she said, 'Be whole-hearted,' and I replied, 'Yes, but...' – one of those 'Yes, but's...' which so frequently came to my lips when talking with Buntie.

And she cut me short at the 'Yes but . . . ' and said, with emphasis, *'Be whole-hearted.''*

And I got her message. When it is being put to you like that, there really isn't any, 'Yes, but . . . '. It's perfectly clear.

*

We talked about my extensive depressions. 'Aren't most people depressed most of the time?' I asked. 'After all, so much of life is depressing.' She shook her head firmly. 'No. Sad perhaps, but not depressing. People feel grief, people feel sorrow, but that is quite, quite different from depression.'

On another occasion she said, 'Suffering is very good. You must suffer,' wanting to make it clear that there was no escape from the true difficulties of life and that no growth could take place without them. She told me about a woman who had some painful misfortunes befall her and came complaining, 'Why me?'

'Why not you?' Buntie had replied.

*

One of the vital aspects of Buntie's teaching was what a friend of mine who had also been one of her pupils once very aptly named – her 'spiritual hand grenades.' There were many of these one-liners, one of which, for example, has supplied the answer to most of my desperate dilemmas time after time: 'Our present circumstances demand exactly the discipline we require at this moment!'

*

Through everything she said or did, Buntie was most interested in the positive, in finding the healthy aspects, the strengths, the gifts of her 'sweethearts' and helping them to grow. She did not shirk the negative. Indeed, she could startle me into recognition of a less than admirable part of myself with a single swift remark. She insisted that one's darker side was an inescapable responsibility, to be known and acknowledged as fully as possible, and her intuitive sense of where the weaknesses lay was as sharp as her sense of hidden vitality. But her emphasis fell, always, on what was most responsive or creative in the self.

Other therapists I had known seemed more interested in sickness, in neurosis, in what didn't function. The object was, or so I thought, to 'cure' these diseased areas so that I could 'function normally.' Buntie cared more about what I could already do well, the directions my deepest passions and impulses took, what I wanted most when not driven and distracted by a relentless sense of duty.

*

The greatest depth of her teaching was that she knew I would only hear when I was ready.

*

When I was lying on the floor sobbing and saying, 'I don't know what I want,' Buntie said, 'Life is not what you want, dearest. Life lives you.'

*

129

I felt drawn to write a book about some work I was doing. My dreams gave me a great deal of confirmation about this. And my fear of failure blocked me. One session I asked, 'Do you think I will ever write this book?'

'It depends on whether you have the courage,' she replied.

'Courage?' I asked, puzzled.

'Spiritual courage,' she said.

*

When I first went to Buntie I rather hoped that she would give me some magic formula for meditation and was rather disappointed when she resisted. However she eventually lent me a record of meditation music which I taped and played every morning when I sat. It was beautiful and haunting, a Japanese instrument and a clarinet which greatly comforted me. I realized however that I was beset with thoughts that were difficult to 'let go' so I pressed her once more and she said, 'You could watch your breath, counting each one until ten and then repeating.' Now I realize that there are many ways to meditate but am grateful for the props she gave me for my path.

*

Buntie was going on a meditation course which sounded grim when she described it to me. When I queried the necessity for her to spend time in such primitive conditions, she said, 'I am always working on myself. I have to keep my mirror clean.'

*

When I was thanking her for all she had done for me, she simply replied, 'I haven't done anything. I am just sitting here as a mirror.'

*

Buntie used to lend books without keeping any record of where they went. If any of them were not eventually returned, she took the attitude that the book was meant to remain with whoever had it, and was more important to that person.

*

Remember how she would get cross at you for attempting to read up about something when she really felt it should have been left to your unconscious experience?

*

It would have been surprising if the Tree of Life had not been an important feature of Buntie's teaching. The symbol was reinforced by her personal experience. She told me that before she started her training Toni had asked her a crucial question: 'The root of a living tree is beneath the pavement. How can it survive?'

Her answer was, 'It breaks through the pavement.'

Even that correct deduction did not touch Buntie as nearly as something she discovered about her living-space.

Before 10a Cunningham Place was built, the workmen had to cut down a tree. For Buntie it still lived: real, like the plants and flowers she tended and loved. That idea found a central place in a poem I wrote to her.

*

131

One day Buntie found the plans for Landseer Studios when it was inhabited by the engraver Landseer and his family. It was the only house in the area: the canal had already been built and grass ran right down to its banks. The studio part of the house was built later, so on the plan that Buntie saw there was a large tree where the studio is now. Whenever I went to see Buntie, I liked to think of sitting in the branches of a tree.

The tree was a very strong, powerful image which she used as a metaphor about life. She saw our choice as growing a tree or climbing a ladder. With the tree, the seasons may change, branches may fall, but the central trunk remains and grows. A ladder is a dangerous thing: it will rot and decay and can collapse under you.

*

She would often say when I spoke about my hopes and ambitions, 'Plant trees, don't put up ladders.'

*

Buntie asked a small gathering, 'What was your vision as a teenager?'

'Mine,' I said, 'was to save the world.'

'You *are* the world,' she said.

*

In an early session with her, she drew for me the Cross. Then she explained how the base of it could grow down through the rubble to the earth, would grow roots, then the Cross could bear leaves, flowers – even fruit, and then, look! no longer a bleak two dimensional diagram but a live, creative, energy-giving symbol.

*

As an intuitive thinker I was having the usual difficulties in knowing what and where my feelings were. Buntie responded by first prodding her own chest at heart level, saying, 'Me,' and then prodding mine and saying, 'You.' She added, 'When we truly respond and understand, we do so from the heart centre and not from the head – it is only then that we exclaim, '*I* see!' or 'I *see!*'

She proceeded to draw the Cross, the one of the tree with its heart in its roots, the roots extending as deep into the earth as the branches rise high into the sky. [An example is included on page five of the photographs and illustrations.]

These powerful images occurring quite naturally and spontaneously in the therapy session have remained an active therapy for me ever since.

*

Ask me about particular memories – oh yes – just the warmth of her hands and the warmth of her eyes when she held my hands and just looked into my face and let me share my pain. And when I left she would call me a 'silly sausage' – and say, 'Bless you.' I love that woman very much. I often remember her advice and wisdom – very simple and very true. Like about new beginnings and change. She said it was like a little seed, not to keep digging it up to see how much it has grown and/or telling everybody about it so it dies in still-birth, but just to nourish it and protect it and give it room to grow.

Her frequent image of trees – of becoming a large tree where other people can shelter underneath and where birds can rest in the branches, was, and is still, an inspiration to me to be likewise.

*

I had worked with Buntie for about two years when I left London and moved to a town just west of it. I was absolutely full of the Buntie teachings – the way of the spiral, and learning lessons from problems.

My new friends began to notice that whenever any of them came to talk something over with me, I nearly always said the same things, always beginning, 'My friend Buntie says . . .' . They started calling me 'B.R.' I eventually persuaded one of them to tell me what the initials stood for – they wouldn't for ages – and she said, 'Buntie Robot.' A few evenings after that we were all in a pub and I asked them what they meant by it. My flat-mate told me that they had all begun to feel fed up at having this Buntie character rammed down their throats. I of course defended myself and jumped in to defend Buntie by explaining how wise she was and how everything she said made such good sense etc. etc. etc. My flat mate said, 'That's fine – for you, but none of us know her and don't want you forcing all this wisdom down our throats.'

Then one of the others said, 'Do you remember when Ron and I split up, I came round to see you one afternoon, all upset and depressed? I know now it wasn't such a big deal – we argued, split up, talked it over and got back together again. But at the time it felt as though my world was falling apart – and all you kept on about was spirals and learning lessons. I was more depressed having talked to you than at the beginning.'

I laughed: it was true, there I was being all wise and wonderful, passing on what I had got from Buntie with a sledgehammer. I remembered then what a boyfriend had said to me when I was going on like this, 'You do realise that I know more about what you believe by how you live than what you say?'

*

I spent a lot of time with the housebound mother of another Buntie pupil. Her mother was both intrigued about our work with Buntie and sceptical, and we would talk about it sometimes. Once she said, 'All of you who come here, you sound like Buntie clones.'

I realized then that I was using Buntie's lovely one-liners and her way of speaking about things rather than digesting them into my own expression.

Buntie had once told me a story about how Jung had stomped out of a banquet when someone started speaking about 'Jungians' because, as he said, anyone who truly understood what he wrote could never be a 'Jungian.' The essence of his teaching about individuation was just that – that you had to find the essence of yourself. I realised that I was in danger of becoming a 'Willsian' – and that she would have been appalled.

*

When I first met Buntie I wasn't immediately aware of her special qualities. Absorbed by my own difficulties, I wondered at first why I was going to see this kindly old lady, every Saturday, miles from where I lived.

As our meetings progressed I began to realise how powerfully compassionate she was. For me this feeling was reinforced by her strong links with Buddhism, and our mutual friends. She became a major catalyst in the solution of many deep-seated problems and my time with her was much too short.

135

She was guru and grandmother to me. It still moves me to tears to think of her and how much I regret that my daughter will never meet her.

*

Buntie sent this on a card to me, 'The wisdom of the Mother dwells in the depths, and to be one with Her means to be granted a vision of deeper things. The roots of the heart spread far and deep.'

*

To listen deeply is
to feel deeply is
to live deeply is
to love deeply is
WHOLENESS is
HOLINESS

ENDING SESSIONS

People remember the way their sessions ended as much as how they began. They were endowed by Buntie with as much warmth as her welcome. She stressed that there was no separation just because the session had ended and the door closed behind you.

*

She said the ring of the doorbell was important because that was often when a session really started. The doorbell made the person with her aware that their session was almost finished. That was part of why *it* happened; you were at the same time under pressure and feeling relief that the session was almost over, so you felt safe, and that's when something would shift or open up.

*

There was always the last ten minutes, and the panic that this whole hour of timelessness, the moment when things made sense, was actually subject to time and was going to end, and the greed to get your full hour. You had started 40 minutes late and you were determined you were going to end 40 minutes late. In time, with Buntie's subtle and silent help, I learned how to handle that last ten minutes. Instead of filling

137

it with questions and a desperate need to have answers, it was best spent in silence. It was so obvious and it took me so long to get there. The sense of 'squandering' that valuable last ten minutes in doing nothing, in not speaking, was heaven.

In Studio E there was a sentence pinned up on the board on the easel. I asked Buntie where it came from and she said it was actually her own. It said: 'In meditation, we have everything to lose and nothing to gain.' And I found it very strengthening to spend that last ten minutes in losing everything and gaining nothing.

*

I recall the hug that came at the end, and at the beginning if I needed two hugs. And asking me to pull her up from chair as if I had a contribution to make.

*

After the end of the session, Buntie would walk with me to the top of the stairs and there was always that hug, the arm around the shoulder, and that was very precious – the strengthening that helped one out into the street again.

*

Did you ever go to Buntie and not meet her? Did you ever feel that the whole hour had been brutally squandered, and that it was your fault? Because I did many times. On one occasion we just didn't seem to meet. I couldn't put into words what I needed to say and Buntie was distracted, and very tired, and seemed to me to be telling me things that lacked the vitality that I needed. On that occasion I came out feeling empty, cross with myself, upset that my precious hour a month with her had been spent in missing each other, in not meeting, and I drove off from Cunningham Place with this distress deep in myself.

I went up to Primrose Hill and I sat down on the grass and I just let it all grow through me and as it did a wonderful realization dawned on me, that this non-meeting was a clumsy illusion by which we fill our lives, that meeting in depth is constantly taking place between us all. We are all one in depth. It was a most wonderful discovery.

I wrote all this to Buntie and one of her American sweethearts who was visiting was sent to deliver by hand a postcard from Buntie with wonderful coloured inks and that splendid writing with huge capital letters:

'Tuesday June 9th, 1981: Letter received.

'My dear: Yes, in depth, all is union, is life, is silence, is light, is truth, is God. Meditate by "breathing in love" and then "breathing out love."

'Love and blessings and support, Buntie.'

*

A friend of mine remembers Buntie saying, at the end of the session, 'This is for *you*,' i.e. digest it yourself, don't blab about it to others.

*

I often wondered how Buntie could end a session with me and go straight on to work with someone else. She took no break. And this went on virtually all day. One day she said to me that if a therapist hadn't found his or her own centre then they could literally be driven mad by the constant stream of their clients' problems. She mentioned that she didn't need to rest between sweethearts because she had learnt not to identify with them.

*

I learned that the time between sessions was as important as the session. One day when I was feeling panicky about it being a week till we met, she said, 'You silly sausage. Do you imagine that we are separate just because you walk out that door?'

Buntie was unwilling to see anyone more than once a week except in the greatest emergency. And she often took at least six weeks of holiday in the summer. As time went on, I slowly became less anxious and more aware of how important for me that 'in between' time was. I could feel the lessons becoming my own; I could hear my own inner voice better, rather than just reacting to Buntie. I listened for my own dreams. And during the holidays I lived a life that was not shaped by those weekly sessions.

I know some of us gave her a hard time about not seeing us more often, or 'abandoning' us in the summer, but I am grateful now for her courage in allowing us our growing space.

*

Pursue your true self
with gentleness and love, patience and courage.

III ABOUT GROUPS

Apart from gathering a wide circle of people around herself, Buntie initiated several groups in Studio E and encouraged others to form their own. They were an important part of her work which benefitted many of her students in diverse and unexpected ways. Groups were invaluable, she said, because, 'All life is relationship.'

*

In the days when Buntie had only the top floor at 10 Cunningham Place, Christmas and Easter 'parties' for the Monday Group necessitated her spending a whole day disrupting and clearing her 'living' room before the event to make sufficient space, and another day afterwards replacing everything, while continuing her normal day's work. But no one would ever have known.

I was present once while Buntie finished arranging the small waiting room which would be used for the meditation and ritual at one of these parties. It was a tight squeeze, and she was eventually left holding a rather large vase with nowhere to put it. There was a pause, then she said, 'I know!' and deposited it unceremoniously outside on the landing, near the door. 'We'll put it here – and they'll all think it's terribly significant!'

*

I once heard Buntie tell us in a group that 'of course all "leaders" are "mis-leaders".' She stated this as if it were something self-evident, which it is. If the Kingdom of Heaven is within us, influence from 'the outside' can only possibly lead us away from it. It is evident that someone else's realization is not a realization of 'The Self.' Indeed there is a danger in my even quoting Buntie's words because of the idea at the back of my mind that Buntie is dead and thus in some sense separated from me here and now. I am also in a sense turning Buntie into a 'leader' somewhere out there and am thus responsible for the error of turning her into a mis- leader and so risking misleading myself and others as well.

*

Buntie Wills' work with groups, like her work with individuals, took its inspiration and direction from a central point of remembering the Self. Many of her own notes reiterated her Teacher's advice to ask, 'who am I?' – a method which contains a way of life and ultimately complete psychological transformation.

The centrality of this Self-based inquiry (unusual in the world of group work) shaped also the physical form of the group – the sitting in a circle around the light of a single candle symbolizing a spiritual centre within each participant which lies beyond their ordinary ego-consciousness.

Group work was conducted to allow each participant in turn to shape the results of their work on themselves – a work which was described as removal of those aspects of conditioning or 'stumbling blocks' which hinder natural development of the personality – the instinct for individuation or 'wholeness' – an aspect of Jungian psychology that Buntie Wills seems most to have embodied in herself and her work with others. Then there were her own written statements which were an effort to express the essence of the Teachings she had made her own through meditation.

Group work with Buntie had a special kind of atmosphere of attention and tension and acceptance: an atmosphere in which there was more emphasis on silence and listening (that listening behind the words by which she set such store) than on discussion. Participants were encouraged to speak but also to listen to what they had themselves said, on the principle that it's only what we learn and can formulate for ourselves which is ultimately transforming for us.

*

I was in the Saturday Group, a study and homework group which suceeded the Monday Group. It seemed to me that Buntie handled it less as an amorphous entity – although its wholeness was very cared for at a spiritual level – but more as a collection of individuals whose psychological needs were all very different. It was rather like a wheel with Buntie holding the centre while each of us was linked in by the spoke of our particular relationship with her; this meant a source of help, nourishment and immediacy but perhaps I sometimes found the interrelating with the others on the rim difficult as the pull to Buntie was so strong.

In some ways the group was much more an extension of my individual work than a new and different learning process. That is not to say that the energy of the group was not powerful and helpful. Buntie's very particular approach with groups seemed to reflect the uncompromising importance she placed on the growth of each Self even at the expense of our occasionally bruised personas.

*

145

Several times at the Saturday Group I had the following experience: The twelve or so of us were sitting in silence waiting for her arrival; then when she came, she also sat in silence with us all for five or ten minutes. I lifted my eyes to take in her stillness and beauty – and I had the deep feeling that we all of us – in spite of our ego-centredness, our muddled shadows, our immaturity – loved her. Once I told her this, and she replied, 'Yes, I know. That's what makes it possible for me to go on.'

*

I asked Buntie if I could come to one of the groups that took place at Studio E, but she said, 'No,' reflectively. 'I don't think it would be a good thing.' I had a great many dreams about it, always arriving at doors and not being allowed in.

*

Two of Buntie's well-known 'spiritual hand grenades' about being in groups have stuck with me ever since. At one session I was describing quite judgementally the backwardness and confusion of one group I had been to. She said, 'Remember, my sweetheart, that it only takes one person in a group who is centred in the Truth to make a difference to the whole group.'

Now, before I am going to a group, whether as a participant or a facilitator, I take a few minutes to meditate on the group. I use something she once taught us: drawing each individual into the light, to the lighted candle at the centre, and then bringing them in turn into your heart. I won't pretend I do this consistently, for I am quite lazy and forgetful spiritually, but when I do, I find that my ego has a healthier relationship to the proceedings.

146

Another time we were discussing some social occasion to which she had had to go. She recounted something Toni had told her, when she was complaining that going to some social do or another was a waste of time. 'There will always be a reason for your being there, other than the reason for which you think you are going.' Time after time this has been confirmed for me, from what seems like the most tedious conference to a social gathering which would otherwise be awkward for me – a meeting in depth, a connection made, someone in need of being listened to.

*

I ran a wide range of groups over the time I worked with Buntie. These included groups on team development and organizational clarity, assertion training and confidence training with teachers, women's groups and teenagers, and groups to help people explore, expand and liberate their musical voices. Buntie had long been encouraging me to focus down and simplify my multifarious activities, and with her help and the help of an unambiguous dream which told me to concentrate on my artistic creative activities, I found myself earning a living by singing and running voice workshops.

Buntie as a visual artist certainly knew about the creative process but nothing as such about voice. And as an individual psychotherapist she had little to offer in the way of formal group training skills. I had acquired these by my own attendance at groups and appropriate training courses. However I owe much of the development and continuing growth of groups I run to what I learned through my time with Buntie. To affirm and trust yet not leave the shadow unacknowledged, to give clear structures and not to be frightened of leaving space and silences, to trust that people are in charge of their own learning and responsible for this at their own pace, to be unapologetically passionate and enthusiastic while not being invasive, these are all ways in which I hope to offer groups their own individual and collective possibility of finding their true voices in depth.

*

Buntie encouraged me when I was doing meditation to set up a women's meditation group. She very much wanted me to continue with the group, because, she said, 'It is important for women to have solidarity in these times, to reinforce the Feminine.'

*

Buntie encouraged a lot of us to support a new international organization called 'Universal Education. It was inaugurated in Italy at a large conference and a number of countries were represented. Groups were initiated that promoted harmonious and holistic education through conferences, workshops, publications, and even through founding their own schools.

I felt so honoured when Buntie suggested that I should take part in this world-wide initiative: it was the epitome of all I had been working for in trying to promote enlightened education on a global scale. Back in Britain we formed a group that ran creative workshops and produced a journal entitled *Educare* and I was privileged to make contact and work with other groups which had sprung up in many parts of the world. For me this was the realization of my deep feelings about the need for a new kind of spiritual education the world over.

*

Everything that Buntie said or did helped me in some way in my work with groups. It wasn't that she ever told me how to run my workshops and seminars. It was to do with giving me an awareness of the precious needs of each and every individual, through her consideration of my own demands. I learned to be really aware of the fact that groups are made up of individuals. As I was listened to, so I began to listen to my students with my heart.

Buntie never directed me when I saw her as an individual, although she could lead me towards the way that was right for me at the time. In the same fashion I learned to sense the direction of a group and ease it towards its own realization. This called for trust on everyone's part, and that was not always immediate. The non-judgemental atmosphere which was so much a part of Buntie's relationship with me and which I tried to create, I know paved the way for each person feeling valued. Just as Buntie knew when we could take something that would be revealing to us, so as the feeling of security developed in a group, I found that the group itself became more open and at the same time more united.

Finally I learned through Buntie the value of being quiet together at the beginning and the ending of a meeting, with a candle flame burning at the centre of the group. There is something magical about a flame which can centre and draw us together.

*

I started seeing Buntie in the winter of 1963 and continued to see her until she died. Some time during the 1960s, I remember her fixing me with that penetrating gaze and saying, 'Dearest –a Norwegian woman who has brought back from China the ancient movements of the T'ai-Chi Ch'uan, is coming here to give a talk and demonstration.'

At that time I was unreceptive to pretty well everything except just staying alive and I wasn't curious. Twice, with several-year intervals, the subject was raised again, each time more firmly. I finally went, but in a very half-hearted fashion. From time to time Buntie would ask me how it was going and I always replied, with more enthusiasm than I genuinely felt, that it was going fine.

Eventually I was persuaded to take part in one of my teacher's weekend workshops. Finding herself with no one to teach the beginners, she asked me to help and I, having nothing to lose, plunged in. From that moment I knew what I wanted to do with my (up till then) aimless life. Being a frustrated dancer and actress, I was overwhelmed with the joy and pleasure of teaching a movement – and a movement of truthfulness and depth containing ancient Chinese philosophy and wisdom.

On returning from the weekend, I couldn't wait for my next 'Buntie lesson.' When it arrived and we were sitting face to face, I must have burst out with my news, that I was going to study properly and teach the T'ai-Chi. There was not a flicker of surprise from her, she just seemed to look into me, for ages, and then I realized her invisible hand at work! She had known what it took me ten years to discover about myself. She immediately made her studio available for me to start my own small classes. I held about four a week up until the time she died and Studio E moved house.

*

She seemed always so thrilled that the studio was being used for groups with a serious and worthwhile endeavour. The rent she asked was ridiculously small, but as we all remember about her, money was very much of secondary importance. She gave me all the encouragement I needed, the encouragement I had lacked in my earlier life. By allowing

150

my groups and others to use the studio with its very special atmosphere and energy, our confidence in ourselves and our abilities was healed and restored.

*

Apart from T'ai-Chi classes, there were other groups, such as the 'Play Reading Group,' which met once a month on a Saturday afternoon, instigated by Buntie and led by a professional actress. As well as being great fun, it had the value of getting shy people like me to use our voices and be heard. A number of Buntie's 'pupils' were lonely and lacking in confidence, so it was an afternoon to meet others as well as sharing the play. There was always a cake so thoughtfully provided for the 'interval,' and a kitchenette for making tea, so it was a social event as well as the interesting experience of exploring different characters. The play to be read was always very carefully chosen to match the number of characters with the available 'cast,' and a lot of energy went into those afternoons.

*

Manjushri London started in Buntie's studio. We wanted to begin a Tibetan Buddhist centre in the city and there was nowhere to go, so Buntie offered her place. We were aware of her generosity, especially as she also gave up her consulting room so that the teacher could meet people privately afterwards. Buntie gave us the opportunity to grow in strength and numbers until we found a new home.

*

A meditation and teaching group started with Buntie's approval on Thursday evenings, led by a man who has since become a poet and therapist. These did not last long and when quite naturally they came to an end, those who had taken part were left with a gap. It was suggested to Buntie that we should go on meeting for an evening of meditation without a leader.

This suggestion was wholeheartedly welcomed and encouraged, the only stipulation being that the evening should finish by 9 p.m. So a very small group, later to become known as the 'Thursday Group' evolved. Because of the organic nature of its beginnings it has endured and flourished, still with its initial strength of purpose. Occasionally a like-minded person has joined, and a very powerful bond has developed amongst the group. It is like a silent foundation on which Buntie's deepest teachings are built. To be unable to attend is to be deprived of nourishment for the coming week.

When Buntie saw that this group had inner discipline and persevered year after year, without a leader and just having a small ritual of a bell rung for beginning and ending the silence, she started to pass to the group cards on which she had written a few sentences distilled from Ramana's teachings, which would be read during the meditation. These cards were kept and copied into a small book and are still read during the Thursday evening meditation.

At the times of great events in the cosmic calendar, such as Christmas Eve and Good Friday, the Thursday Group is open to anyone at Studio E who is able and wishes to spend time significantly, perhaps just fifteen minutes snatched from a busy day, or several hours. During these times the sittings are punctuated by readings that Buntie gave over the years. Some are her own profoundly intuited truths, others are from different spiritual teachers.

*

Of all the groups, the one that gave her the deepest and purest joy was the Ramana Group. This came about near the end of her life. For some years there had been an altar in the Studio, discreetly placed behind a curtain and covered with

152

a beautiful cloth donated by a 'pupil' on which sat a Buddha, a photo of Sri Ramana Maharshi, a bell brought back from a Zen monastery in Japan by another pupil, and always, fresh flowers. Incidentally, this tradition started by Buntie lives on in the present Studio E.

From *The Mountain Path*, the magazine circulated from the Ramanashramam in South India, Buntie read that a meditation group following the teachings of Ramana was forming in London. She offered the studio as a regular meeting place, and monthly meetings there were led by someone who had been a devotee of Ramana's since the age of 14 when he went to the Ashram, on leave from the Air Force Cadets, and sat at Ramana's feet. This direct link with the Guru charged the meetings and meditations in the studio with great spiritual depth.

Buntie was radiant; she attended some meetings, but sometimes chose to stay in her room and be with the group in spirit. One of my last remembrances of her was standing with her in the hallway and although she looked frail and exhausted she also looked wonderfully happy. She told me how she had made the altar six years previously and waited And at last someone had come from Ramana.

*

The largest group of all arose out of Buntie's death. As her illness progressed in the autumn of 1985 and it became clear that she was not going to recover, she suggested ways in which the work could go on. She was aware that her rooms and Studio E were likely to be lost – her landlord had other plans for the property and had had his eye on her rooms for years. She was happy, whatever happened about 10a Cunningham Place, that some sort of organization would be formed and that all the marvellous creative energy around Cunningham Place not be allowed to disperse and simply peter out.

153

What Buntie had suspected did come to pass: a few months after her death, her rooms and Studio E had to be vacated. Groups met temporarily in assorted places – school rooms, church halls, homes – while a small group of people tried to find alternative premises. Finally the beautiful flat at 49 The Avenue was offered – the result of a bedside meeting the day before Buntie died, between a hospital volunteer who just happened to be an ex-pupil, Buntie's sister, and one of Buntie's secretaries. As Buntie had been known to say of similar meetings, 'Not by accident, my sweethearts, but by appointment.'

In fact, the premises were rather larger and more spacious than the small group who helped clear Cunningham Place had in mind, but then one of Buntie's long-term pupils offered to guarantee the rent. In early March 1986, a meeting took place to look at ways in which 49 The Avenue could become financially feasible. It was decided to try to form a charitable trust, and out of this grew the shape and form of The Buntie Wills Foundation.

It was Buntie's wish that her library should be available to a former pupil who had become a Jungian analyst, and her paintings and pottery were given to the Foundation by her executors, her sister Jennie and her friend Gabrielle Boole, along with some of the furniture and objects which had made Cunningham Place so distinctive. People frequently comment that the very atmosphere of the old studio seems to have transferred itself with them. There is little doubt that the spirit Buntie fostered in smaller groups also pervades the much larger group of the Foundation which eventually arose out of them.

*

When a form in the first newsletter from the Foundation asked people to indicate which suggested activities or groups they might be interested in, I was immediately attracted to being part of a group which 'did a book about Buntie, having developed my own writing under her encouragement. But I suspect that none of us who came to the first gathering of the Books Group in November 1986 would have turned up if we could have known we were beginning a four-year task!

We were a mixed set whose number varied in the early meetings, but has been constant for the past three and a half years. We were nearly all strangers to each other then, and still do not meet socially. Some of us had experience of writing or editing, others just wanted to make sure something got written. Some had been part of one group or another around Buntie, others not at all.

At first I felt some reluctance at giving up my 'precious Sundays' but as our work got under way I found that the group and its task became such a rewarding and integral part of my life that I would not consider missing a meeting, even under severe domestic pressure.

It still amazes me that such a motley assortment of us came to work so well together, but I realize that a very real cohesion grew gradually over the years. We met on Sundays at Studio E, usually every three months or so, and perhaps our shared picnic lunches are a good example of that cohesion. Our individual spontaneous contributions to them emerged every time, without fail, as a well-balanced feast that couldn't have been better if planned!

This kind of 'going together' became a frequent occurrence in the work of the group, and whenever we recognized it anew, we felt it showed that we were on course. It happened in so many ways.

We started meetings with a short silence round a lighted candle. Then we took it in turn to 'check in, telling how and where we were in our lives. Sometimes this took an hour, sometimes fifteen minutes. We shared with the others whatever we wanted to: a new kitchen or a new insight, it did not matter. What did seem to matter a great deal to the work that followed was that we had taken the time to do so. Having each of our voices and stories heard seemed to set a pattern of sharing for the rest of the day's work.

I continue to marvel at how the work got done. None of us is exactly retiring or reticent; we are each used to really 'doing our own thing.' We have had quite strong and sometimes very different ideas about various aspects of the books. The meetings were not quiet, but they were also full of laughs, and they developed an atmosphere in which I think we were not afraid to speak our honest opinions and to listen totally to others doing the same, in the service of a shared task and a deep purpose. In so doing we arrived each time at a resolution that suited everyone: a resolution which was more than the sum of its parts, and always seemed slightly miraculous in its arrival.

We discovered that our tasks – preparing *The Tree of Life* talks as well as this book – grew in their own time. When we decided to tackle first the Buntie book, as we called this one, there weren't enough contributions and we had to start on the Tree of Life book too. A year later a flood of contributions swept the Buntie book forward just as the first stage of work on the Tree talks was completed. We found that when work on one lacked a sense of direction, it was because it was time to attend to the other. When we decided to have a final section relating to Buntie's death, we set a meeting to discuss only that subject, because we realized how important it was to us all for a variety of reasons. But on the day we ran into such a shared block that we just had to say, 'It's not the time.' Work progressed on other areas for a while, until one day we sensed that we could try again – this time the discussion flowed like a river.

People in the group have also had their own time in the scheme of things. It hasn't been a group where a few people did all the work and the others just came for the lunch. As it turns out, the particular vision, skill or talent of each one of us became just what was needed by all, but at different stages in the preparation. Ideas people, form-and-shapers, critics, practical people, those with publishing or printing knowledge, patient ones and speedy ones – we needed them all, and as it turned out we had them.

All the work was done in full reference to the whole group. No stage went forward without the concurrence of all. Even when time pressure broke up tasks to be done by individuals, the results were always reviewed jointly. That was the pattern which showed itself to be the right way for us to proceed – and somehow time always seemed to accommodate it.

Committing ourselves to the final title was perhaps the hardest task, and on that occasion time helped by working against us. We had spent seven hours on final editing, and there were only five minutes before one member had to leave to catch a train. We had fifteen different – really different – suggestions in front of us. We set about them as we had learned to do, first working out the principles – that we wanted a title both informative and suggestive, so that a stranger seeing it on a shelf would get some information and also be intrigued enough to open the book. Then we tossed around our feelings in the light of this principle, playing with individual words – and suddenly there it was, the solution. At just the right moment.

Looking back, it was as though we had been weaving a long carpet. We had our heads down, working away stitch by stitch, and now and again when we raised our heads and looked, there suddenly was a pattern to see. It was an amazing experience being part of all that.

Now that our 'carpet' is complete, I wonder how it will feel to see the completed task physically, to hold the two books in our hands. We know that not everyone will like the way we have done them, and we are prepared to accept that. We know, too, that we will miss our meetings together, so we will need to look as individuals at whether we have a future as a group, or whether it is time to let go. We have set aside time to consider all this. My own deep love for us all, and the experience of the process that we have shared, give me trust that these questions will also reach their true resolution.

*

*Group relationships may take various forms,
each of which has its value, all of which are to be sought.
Everything depends on the relationship being made in depth.*

P.W. Martin

IV ON LIFE AND DEATH

On a certain occasion I was trying to express to Buntie my fear of death. She sat very still and then quietly, simply and almost casually said, 'When someone says they are afraid of dying, the actual fact is that they are afraid of living.'

*

I phoned Buntie all in a tizz. I was convinced I was dying. Buntie said, 'Yes dearest, perhaps you are. But your time of death is already set. So just get on with living.'

*

When Buntie phoned to tell me that a mutual friend had just died, I asked whether she had been with her. She said, 'Yes, we made the journey together.' Later, Buntie was to die in the same place herself. Perhaps her experience with this friend was a preparation for her own journey later.

*

An important part of Buntie's death, for me, was the fact that everything in her life was already coming to an end. The house was falling to bits and pressure was about to be brought on her tenancy by the landlord. Some of us wondered anyway how she could survive another winter there. Her secretary had left, and a long-time group had disbanded. The path was already downhill.

*

In my very last session with Buntie, she had a really bad chest and a terrible cough. She told me she was not well. I felt she was really saying, 'My time is finished . . . ' .

*

I found it really difficult not to have any contact with Buntie in the last months before she died. I resented not knowing what was going on.

*

I understood that Buntie was an intensely private person and respected her need to be alone with her illness. She too was on a path and probably had unfinished business to deal with.

*

Buntie had encouraged me to set up a women's meditation group. When she was ill, in order not to encroach upon the very private world of her illness, I wrote her a pseudo-jokey letter which also asked if there was anything I could do. She replied in a matching light vein, but adding a very strong request, that 'the most helpful thing you can do is remember me in your meditations with the women.'

*

Most people are too clogged up with their own lives really to see out. Buntie led me to realize that one must strive to shake off self like a skin that blinds one from seeing into the kernel of things and helping others. When she was ill, I was away from London. I followed her illness from afar, hearing when she had gone into the hospice. Days passed. Suddenly I got a letter from her. It gave me a great shock, for I thought she was dead. I opened it as if it was a message from heaven. It was very short. She said, 'Hold on to perception. It is the most precious gift of all, but it must be accompanied by humility.'

*

I was saddened to learn that Buntie did not have a very easy time before her death. I felt that her great heart and giving nature might have deserved better. But the Tree of Life helped me to understand that a developed person such as she became, living directly out of the inner self, has essentially the attribute of devotion to the Work. That is certainly true of Buntie. And inherent in that devotion is its opposite – pride; they cannot be separated. It seemed clear to me then that any difficulties she experienced of pride or anger during the course of her illness were a very necessary and integral part of her living the life of the spirit to the last.

*

I was very glad to learn that at the very end in the hospice, Buntie was in good enough form in herself to joke with the nurses.

*

On the morning of December 9th, I woke at 4.30 a.m. My head was in a wind, and I thought, 'Buntie is on Arunachala,' the Holy Mountain where Ramana had lived. It was later that morning that I got the phone call telling me that she had died.

*

Buntie was alone at the actual moment of her death. Perhaps she chose to be. This occurred to me when I found the following story:

'A Zen master calligrapher was sketching an important phrase accompanied by a bold pupil who never failed to criticize his master's work.

"That is not good," he told the Master after the first effort.

"How is that one?"

"Poor. Worse than before," pronounced the pupil.

'The Master patiently wrote one sheet after another until eighty-four had accumulated, still without the approval of the pupil. Then, when the young man stepped outside for a few moments, the Master thought, "Now is my chance to escape his keen eye," and he wrote the phrase hurriedly with a mind free from distraction.

"A masterpiece," pronounced the pupil.'

*

I felt very angry when she died. I put off accepting it. The fact that 'she' was growing in me took me many years to acknowledge. I was angry – *why did she smoke?* Why didn't she eat properly? I was being an angry child.

164

*

I have to admit having felt that her death didn't really matter. In fact, I almost didn't go to the big memorial service because I had been invited to a wedding. It was a toss-up. I honestly didn't feel sad. It was as though it were just fine, completely normal. I still feel her presence around.

*

The teacher has to die so that the teaching can take root in ourselves. When the therapist dies, we can no longer have her outside ourselves. We have to take up the process. It also seemed to me that many who were closely connected to her received some of her power and strength.

*

I used to go round to Cunningham Place just to see it. I was a real nuisance at one point. At the beginning of December I suddenly sent Buntie a card of Coventry, a memory of a happy day we had once had together there. I should have known something was wrong when I got no reply. Eventually when I went round there, the blind with the sun on it, which was always in the window, had gone. A wardrobe of Buntie's was in the street. I felt desolate at the time, because I felt that nobody had bothered to tell me. I felt left out of it all. And seeing that wardrobe made me feel that Buntie was being abandoned. Being in the Foundation and in the Books Group, I have found the connection again and no longer feel desolate.

*

It took a long while for my grief to break through. I had to go to an osteopath recently. After he had treated my back, he asked, 'What do you think the problem *really* is?' I found myself crying and crying and crying and then I felt whole. As Buntie would say, 'Don't mind the tears. The river of life is flowing again.'

*

I was told that people were gathering at the old Studio E on the same day as her funeral, which was private. It was the first time I was invited to a group there. Some beautiful readings had been chosen. I felt a belonging more than I'd ever known.

*

Just after Buntie's death a friend shared an image with me. He said he pictured Buntie as a huge and colourful hot air balloon, waiting to be free. We were all the guy ropes holding her to the ground, gradually letting go and allowing her to float away.

A few days later, walking the dogs across the fields, I heard the unmistakable sound of – a hot air balloon. Majestically it passed slowly overhead and then away to the horizon. It seemed like a gift.

*

I thought I had finished grieving for Buntie until quite recently when, feeling upset, I gave myself some space – and suddenly I burst into tears. I asked myself why I was crying and Buntie came into my mind. I said to her, 'I miss you – you were the only person I've ever totally trusted.' This in itself was quite a revelation. Even though there were times when

I'm sure her advice was not fool-proof, I had trusted her integrity. 'So where does this leave me?' I asked myself. Then came the words, 'Trust in your Self.'

Since then I've felt a sort of strength and the influence of her teaching working at some level in me – even when life hasn't been easy. It's in me and I have to live it myself.

*

Thank you so much for having Buntie's Memorial Service invitation sent to me. I thought about it and then felt it would not be right for me to go. This is a big thing with many followers who knew each other, and in some way it represents exactly the opposite of what Buntie was to me. She was the instrument geared to produce big changes in my life and in me, and although I had no contact with her any more, these changes were set and firmly set. They were a road – to introversion, to happenings inside, to developments that have nothing to do with crowds and jubilation. The picture I see of Buntie through this is someone who sparked off lights in millions of people and became a charismatic leader.

It always surprises me, in these modern times, the emphasis on jubilation for lives that are gone. Is it a way to counteract the grief of the lack?

I treasure the memory of Buntie as someone I met at the right time for a purpose – and then lost – but also, through the loss, gained understanding.

*

When I was eight years old, one of my school mates died; this was the first time that I had any contact with death. I became very depressed, triggered off by singing a hymn in the church the Sunday following her death, the one that ends with:

167

'Time like an ever-rolling stream,
Bears all its sons away.
They fly forgotten as a dream
Dies at the opening day.'

Tears down my cheeks echoed 'the ever-rolling stream'
and when it came to:

'A thousand ages in thy sight
Are like an evening gone,'

my grief knew no bounds.

I couldn't explain it to puzzled parents, who tried hard to
find a logical explanation and even bought me a bed of my
own as they were convinced it was all because of having to
share a bed.

Sixty years later Buntie was saying, 'It doesn't matter, they
will come back,' when I confessed shamefacedly that they –
my dreams – had 'flown at the opening day.' And so they did.
I painted them and overcame my deep fear of guilt when
they escaped me.

When Buntie died, off went my dreams on their morning
flight again. A year later, I suddenly thought to myself, 'I
really must remember my dreams,' and felt it in my heart that
night before I went to bed.

In the morning there were lovely dreams all captured in
memory. I had met my long-departed parents in a warm and
caring atmosphere. From then on I have had the possibility
of linking my inner and outer life. It doesn't always work, of
course, but when it doesn't, I hear the words, 'Never mind,
they will come back.'

*

I was a 'novice' in the early 1970s when I came to see Buntie, with little sensing of what was moving either inside or outside me – but Buntie's teachings, the work, the encouragement, the gentle guidings return and move in me more now, since her death, than ever they did then.

*

I learned something from Buntie just recently. I went to see the enthronement of the little Spanish boy who was the reincarnation of Lama Yeshe, a Tibetan lama who Buntie had known well for years. It was a long journey to India and Tibet and nothing was working out.

My life has been filled with form and shape; I am extremely disciplined and I like things to work very methodically and if they don't, I get very, very irritated.

In the middle of Tibet I had a dream. Buntie and Lama Yeshe were together in a vast theatre, and they were putting on a comic-opera. They were standing in the dress circle like a couple of impresarios, both of them middle-aged, and Buntie looking just as she did when she was alive. There were various lamas dashing on and off the stage – and the whole thing was completely ridiculous. I looked down and said, 'What is this opera called?' And I saw it was 'Rigoletto.'

The next morning I told the dream to a friend, and he said, 'You know what it means. It's Wriggle-let-go.' It was my whole, uncomfortable journey. I had to wriggle – and let go.

It was Buntie, still wry, stylish, original – and still teaching.

*

Throughout the years I knew her, I was aware that the teachings Buntie gave us through the spoken word were of importance beyond value. Yet her greatest teachings were conveyed through silence. More even than by anything she said or did, we were changed in depth by the pure essence of her inner stillness.

When in 1985 she died, we lost her bodily presence. We have not lost her silence. The essential teachings are still being imparted . . . constantly. We need only listen with *a good heart.*

*

Buntie gave me life; she is busy now giving me death. Her teaching is preparing me for the experience that will soon be mine, too.

*

Buntie was able to give real substance to my own intuitive awareness that there was very little difference between life and death. She showed me how every night when we go into deep, dreamless sleep we enter a state of 'death' – which we consciously experience but forget on waking – and how every morning when we wake up we re-enter the limited and finite state we call 'life.' I shall never forget the direct, penetrating look and the urgent candour in her voice as she said, 'There is really only one dream.'

I gained from Buntie an increasing awareness that the 'real world' on which we put so much emphasis was, in her words, 'just the tip of the iceberg.' Seven-eighths of an iceberg's form lies below the surface of the ocean and is invisible – and therefore mostly uncredited by us, if not by the iceberg.

Even our experience of tidal movement between waking and sleeping, life and death, and between the tip of the iceberg and its greater substance is true only within its own limitations. While we sleep the world goes about its business

170

and while, in our waking hours, we are small-mindedly absorbed, the limitless world of the 'dead' is constantly, unfailingly present.

In her lifetime Buntie gave us her wholehearted assurance that although physically parted from her we could always call on her for help, guidance and support – and reminded us that we were never separated from her or the teachings just because we had walked out through the door. I feel she gives that assurance even now – the event of death notwithstanding.

*

Someone who comes to the new Studio E but never knew Buntie had a dream recently in which she found a little note that Buntie had pinned to the wall at the Studio. It said, *All will be well.*

*

There has been a series of changes for me since Buntie's death. It has been a gradual process, first of feeling abandoned, which has been a characteristic of mine since early childhood. She had not been able to contact me on the last day I should have seen her and so I was greeted at the doorstep by the secretary who said that Buntie had had to go to the doctor. I never saw her again. I refused to believe that she would leave us and even when a letter came round suggesting other therapists, I thought that I wouldn't ever want anyone else and would be quite prepared to wait until she was better. It was only when a personal reply to my letter started with the words, 'I am really very ill. . . ' that it dawned on me that she might really be dying. I didn't read the rest of the letter; I didn't want to know.

Later, when she died, I wanted to attach myself to a group that was close to her and I wept every time I went past St. John's Wood Road. Some time after that there was a stage

171

when I was very angry with her for going, although I hardly dared admit it to myself. I picked on one piece of advice which she had given me and I felt was wrong. I think I was probably too harsh in the immediate circumstances, but taking a long look at it, she may have been right. In any case, she could have been fallible or I could have interpreted her remarks too literally.

So what has changed since is a long journey towards inner contentment, being able to appreciate what she meant to me as a living part of my life. It is strange that only now, after so many years, can I reap the true benefits of her love and guidance.

I now see more clearly that it was time to be weaned; I wasn't young when I first came to her and she would occasionally refer to the fact that it was high time to grow up! This was said so lovingly and with such humour that I could not help laughing at myself.

Knowing Buntie has set me on a path that I will not relinquish, a rough and stony path but one that leads to a clear light in the future.

*

Although sometimes Buntie used to talk to us about her work as a psychotherapist and its spin-off into the groups that took place in Studio E, I knew little of what went on there, and though occasionally I heard names mentioned in passing I had no idea who they belonged to – whether patients or members of a group or both; I simply thought of them as 'Buntie's people.'

Since her death however, through having been invited to become a Trustee of the Buntie Wills Foundation and going to meetings and social gatherings at Studio E, I have been able to match these ephemeral names to faces and personalities. It was as though a blind had been suddenly raised and there they all were, in quite surprising variety but each with a certain distinctive quality which seemed to tie in with the impressions I had gathered. I had heard about the close friendships that had grown up between them and how they supported each other through illness and other tribulations, and since coming to know them I have become aware how pervasive is this concern for those around them – perhaps a legacy from Buntie?

*

I had a dream recently, and by now Buntie has been dead almost three years. In the dream I wandered into Landseer Studios and found that it had been torn apart by property developers. The place had been stripped, walls were missing and plumbing exposed. The whole of the first floor had been opened up, the dividing walls removed and the remaining walls were bare brick and mortar. The floor was covered with rubble and dust.

I was astonished to see that Buntie was teaching in amongst all this. With all the interior walls gone, there was much more room and I noticed that she was teaching not from the corner where her consulting room had been but from the opposite corner in her private room where her bed had been and the place where she meditated each morning and evening. Amongst the large crowd of pupils were people I had known from the old days, but also people I did not know, who had become her pupils since her death.

My first thoughts were: Why had no-one told me she had returned and was teaching? How could I have misunderstood things so and been ignorant of something of such importance? The clear point of the dream was that Buntie was very much alive and in the body again and quietly teaching – as ever. No carefully cultivated meditative image this – no cherished memory, thinning and half lost, but an utterly real Buntie – 'here and now.'

The discovery made my heart leap with a thrilling burst of excitement and joy. It would no longer be simply a matter of re-reading the notes and trying to remember. Wonderfully, here was real evidence, accidently discovered, that Buntie was active among us all, teaching as ever and, as ever, without heralding or fuss.

The dream was the confirmation I had needed of something I had known in my heart was so.

*

Let me respectfully remind you:
Life and death are of extreme importance.
Do not squander your lives.